Abortion

OPPOSING VIEWPOINTS®

Other Books of Related Interest

Opposing Viewpoints Series

Adoption
American Values
America's Children
America's Future
America's Victims
Biomedical Ethics
Child Abuse
Culture Wars
Death and Dying
The Death Penalty
Euthanasia
The Family in America
Feminism
Genetic Engineering
Health Care in America
Human Sexuality
Illegal Immigration
Male/Female Roles
Population
Poverty
Sexual Values
Teenage Sexuality
21st Century Earth
Violence

Current Controversies Series

The Abortion Controversy
Ethics
Family Violence
Illegal Immigration
Reproductive Technologies
Sexual Harassment
Violence Against Women

At Issue Series

Rape on Campus
What Is Sexual Harassment?

Abortion

OPPOSING VIEWPOINTS®

David Bender & Bruno Leone, *Series Editors*

Tamara L. Roleff, *Book Editor*

OPPOSING
VIEWPOINTS®
SERIES

Greenhaven Press, Inc., San Diego, CA

Photo credit: Gazelle Technologies

Greenhaven Press, Inc.
PO Box 289009
San Diego, CA 92198-9009

Library of Congress Cataloging-in-Publication Data

Abortion : opposing viewpoints / Tamara L. Roleff, book editor.
    p.   cm. — (Opposing viewpoints series)
   Includes bibliographical references and index.
   ISBN 1-56510-506-0 (lib. bdg. : alk. paper). —
ISBN 1-56510-505-2 (pbk. : alk. paper)
    1. Abortion—United States—Moral and ethical aspects.
    2. Abortion—Law and legislation—United States. I. Roleff,
Tamara L., 1959–   . II. Series: Opposing viewpoints series
(Unnumbered)
HQ767.5.U5A266   1997
363.4'6—dc20   96-17342
                                             CIP

"Congress shall make no law . . .
abridging the freedom of speech,
or of the press."

First Amendment to the U.S. Constitution

The basic foundation of our democracy is the First Amendment guarantee of freedom of expression. The Opposing Viewpoints Series is dedicated to the concept of this basic freedom and the idea that it is more important to practice it than to enshrine it.

Contents

Why Consider Opposing Viewpoints?

"The only way in which a human being can make some approach to knowing the whole of a subject is by hearing what can be said about it by persons of every variety of opinion and studying all modes in which it can be looked at by every character of mind. No wise man ever acquired his wisdom in any mode but this."

John Stuart Mill

In our media-intensive culture it is not difficult to find differing opinions. Thousands of newspapers and magazines and dozens of radio and television talk shows resound with differing points of view. The difficulty lies in deciding which opinion to agree with and which "experts" seem the most credible. The more inundated we become with differing opinions and claims, the more essential it is to hone critical reading and thinking skills to evaluate these ideas. Opposing Viewpoints books address this problem directly by presenting stimulating debates that can be used to enhance and teach these skills. The varied opinions contained in each book examine many different aspects of a single issue. While examining these conveniently edited opposing views, readers can develop critical thinking skills such as the ability to compare and contrast authors' credibility, facts, argumentation styles, use of persuasive techniques, and other stylistic tools. In short, the Opposing Viewpoints Series is an ideal way to attain the higher-level thinking and reading skills so essential in a culture of diverse and contradictory opinions.

In addition to providing a tool for critical thinking, Opposing Viewpoints books challenge readers to question their own strongly held opinions and assumptions. Most people form their opinions on the basis of upbringing, peer pressure, and personal, cultural, or professional bias. By reading carefully balanced opposing views, readers must directly confront new ideas as well as the opinions of those with whom they disagree. This is not to simplistically argue that everyone who reads opposing views will—or should—change his or her opinion. Instead, the series enhances readers' depth of understanding of their own views by encouraging confrontation with opposing ideas. Careful examination of others' views can lead to the readers' understanding of the logical inconsistencies in their own opinions, perspective on why they hold an opinion, and the consideration of the possibility that their opinion requires further evaluation.

Evaluating Other Opinions

To ensure that this type of examination occurs, Opposing Viewpoints books present all types of opinions. Prominent spokespeople on different sides of each issue as well as well-known professionals from many disciplines challenge the reader. An additional goal of the series is to provide a forum for other, less known, or even unpopular viewpoints. The opinion of an ordinary person who has had to make the decision to cut off life support from a terminally ill relative, for example, may be just as valuable and provide just as much insight as a medical ethicist's professional opinion. The editors have two additional purposes in including these less known views. One, the editors encourage readers to respect others' opinions—even when not enhanced by professional credibility. It is only by reading or listening to and objectively evaluating others' ideas that one can determine whether they are worthy of consideration. Two, the inclusion of such viewpoints encourages the important critical thinking skill of objectively evaluating an author's credentials and bias. This evaluation will illuminate an author's reasons for taking a particular stance on an issue and will aid in readers' evaluation of the author's ideas.

As series editors of the Opposing Viewpoints Series, it is our hope that these books will give readers a deeper understanding of the issues debated and an appreciation of the complexity of even seemingly simple issues when good and honest people disagree. This awareness is particularly important in a democratic society such as ours in which people enter into public debate to determine the common good. Those with whom one disagrees should not be regarded as enemies but rather as people whose views deserve careful examination and may shed light on one's own.

Thomas Jefferson once said that "difference of opinion leads to inquiry, and inquiry to truth." Jefferson, a broadly educated man, argued that "if a nation expects to be ignorant and free . . . it expects what never was and never will be." As individuals and as a nation, it is imperative that we consider the opinions of others and examine them with skill and discernment. The Opposing Viewpoints Series is intended to help readers achieve this goal.

David L. Bender & Bruno Leone,
Series Editors

Introduction

*"I'm not saying that what I did was legal, but
I'm saying what I did was moral."*
>   Paul Hill, convicted of murdering abortion
>   doctor John Britton and escort James Barrett

*"While there are two sides to the issue of
abortion, there are no two sides to the issue
of shooting people for their opinions."*
> Eleanor Smeal, president of the Fund for the Feminist Majority

The abortion controversy can easily be broken down into two distinct camps: those who oppose abortion and call themselves pro-life and those who support abortion rights and call themselves pro-choice. Abortion rights advocates contend that women have the right to control their bodies by choosing to terminate unwanted pregnancies. Many pro-choice activists insist that this right is absolute and should not be restricted in any manner. Abortion opponents maintain that a fetus's right to life is more important than a woman's right to control her reproduction. For many pro-life activists no reason—including rape, incest, or the health of the mother—justifies abortion. Although in recent years some abortion rights advocates and opponents have searched for common ground, the majority on both sides assert that there can be no compromise. The intractability of each side's position often finds expression in bitter and inflammatory rhetoric. Sometimes the rhetoric leads to violence, usually directed against abortion clinics and providers, but occasionally against abortion protesters.

Since the 1980s, the abortion protests have escalated from peaceful sidewalk picketing to clinic blockades, harassment of clinic workers and patients, vandalism, and bombings. Since 1993, five doctors and clinic workers have been murdered by anti-abortion activists, and one abortion protester claims he has received a death threat in retaliation for the murders. The first murder occurred in March 1993 when Michael Griffin shot doctor and abortion provider David Gunn in Pensacola, Florida. In July 1994, Paul Hill killed abortion provider John Britton and his unarmed escort, James Barrett, and wounded Barrett's wife, June.

The most deadly attack at an abortion clinic to date occurred in December 1994 when John C. Salvi III shot and killed Shannon Lowney and Leanne Nichols, receptionists at two abortion clinics in Brookline, Massachusetts, and wounded five bystanders.

These killers and their supporters argue that the deaths of the doctors and clinic workers should be considered "justifiable homicide." Doctors who perform abortions are serial killers, the protesters maintain, so killing abortion providers saves the lives of babies who otherwise would have been murdered by abortion. Thirty anti-abortion activists signed a letter written by Paul Hill in 1993 that stated:

> The justice of taking godly action necessary to defend innocent life includes the use of force. We proclaim that whatever force is legitimate to defend the life of a born child is legitimate to defend the life of an unborn child.

Donald Spitz, a former Pentecostal minister who heads the anti-abortion group Pro-Life Virginia and who signed Hill's letter, defends the justifiable homicide theory: "If there was a sniper in the schoolyard sniping off children one by one and the only way you could stop him was by stopping that sniper you would stop that sniper."

Abortion rights organizations maintain that Salvi, Hill, Griffin, and others are part of a widespread conspiracy of violence directed by pro-life organizations against abortion clinics and their employees. To support their contention, they point out that many of the violent anti-abortion activists are known to visit or write each other, often before one of them bombs or vandalizes a clinic or shoots a doctor. Nicki Nichols Gamble, president of the Planned Parenthood League of Massachusetts, said after the Brookline clinics murders, "There is no question in my mind that there is a national if not an international network of people who talk to each other, share strategies, share rhetoric and share a perception" that violence against abortion providers is acceptable. The federal government is taking the charges of conspiracy seriously; it has ordered the FBI and the Bureau of Alcohol, Tobacco, and Firearms (ATF) to investigate the anti-abortion movement.

Abortion rights activists also contend that even if no actual conspiracy exists, the inflammatory rhetoric of anti-abortion organizations inspires their followers to commit acts of violence and terrorism. They cite the creed of Randall Terry, founder of Operation Rescue, who urges his followers, "If you believe abortion is murder, then act like it is," as a prime example of such violence-instigating rhetoric. "These people know that as long as they say abortion is murder and it's therefore justified to shoot an abortion doctor, somebody will act it out," maintains Cheryl Glenn, a special agent with the ATF who investigates abortion clinic violence. Some organizations not only justify violence against abortion clinics and providers, argue supporters of abortion rights, but they give their followers instructions on how to carry out such acts. These instructions are found in such publications as *The Army of God*, a manual for anti-abortion activists that describes how to sabotage clinics, and Michael Bray's *A Time to Kill*, which exhorts its readers to commit violence against abortion doctors. Such rhetoric, abortion rights activists maintain, encourages violence against doctors, patients, and clinic workers.

Although Salvi, Hill, Griffin, Spitz, and others categorize themselves as pro-life activists, mainstream pro-life organizations such as the National Right to Life Committee, the American Life League, the Pro-Life Action League, and Operation Rescue National have officially condemned violence against clinic workers. "[Salvi's] shooting is a lawless act, regardless of . . . what his motive was. . . . Violence is not a solution to the abortion tragedy," maintains Paige Cunningham, president of Americans United for Life. Judie Brown, president of the American Life League, concurs. "The taking of a fellow human being's life is wrong. . . . It is not the province of any one of us to somehow justify a brutally sinful act against another's right to life."

The mainstream pro-life movement's leaders also contend that Salvi, Hill, and Griffin were acting on their own rather than with the sanction of the pro-life movement when they shot abortion doctors and clinic employees. Wanda Franz, president of the National Right to Life Committee, asserts:

> We are opposed to having our members engage in any kind of illegal activity. This is just one . . . peripheral issue that involves a very small proportion of fringe people who have nothing to do with the mainstream pro-life movement.

Even the supporters of abortion violence maintain that those who act against the clinics do so independently. While Spitz admits to knowing, meeting with, and supporting the actions of the convicted murderers, he contends that they are not members of a conspiracy nor have they ever discussed the issue of violence against abortion providers during their conversations.

The extreme polarity of views concerning violence against abortion providers is also found in other areas of the abortion debate. *Abortion: Opposing Viewpoints* explores some of the contentious issues surrounding abortion in the following chapters: Is Abortion Immoral? Should Abortion Be Restricted? Can Abortion Be Justified? Is Abortion Safe for Women? Is Research Using Aborted Fetal Tissue Ethical? In this anthology authors discuss the rights, morality, and ethics involved in this emotional and increasingly violent controversy.

Is Abortion Immoral?

Abortion

Chapter Preface

One of the most controversial issues of the abortion debate is the question of when life begins. Many abortion opponents contend that life begins at conception. Any process that terminates a pregnancy after a sperm has fertilized an egg cell—including some birth control methods, such as the IUD, RU 486, and "morning-after" pills—is murder, they argue. Jerome Lejeune, a French pediatrician and geneticist, testified at a U.S. Senate Judiciary Committee hearing that "after fertilization has taken place a new human being has come into being. . . . [This] is no longer a matter of taste or opinion. . . . It is plain experimental evidence." Therefore, he asserts, abortion at any stage of pregnancy kills a human child.

Although some abortion rights activists concede that a zygote or embryo has the potential for human life, they insist that it is not yet a person. Paul D. Simmons, author of *Birth and Death: Bioethical Decision Making*, illustrates this point by comparing a human egg cell with a chicken's egg: "Few of us are confused about what we are eating when we have eggs for breakfast. An egg—even a fertilized egg—is still an egg and not a chicken." Similarly, he contends, a zygote is alive and belongs to the species *homo sapiens*, but it is not a separate human being. Simmons maintains that a zygote merely consists of a few cells and has none of the qualities necessary for personhood, such as self-awareness, moral perception, and social experience. Other abortion rights activists argue that human life is not present until after a fetus reaches viability. Therefore, they assert, abortion of a nonviable fetus is not murder or an otherwise immoral act.

The question of when life begins is just one of the moral issues involved in the controversy over abortion. In the following chapter, theologians, physicians, and abortion rights supporters and opponents debate whether abortion is moral, whether it is a selfish choice, and whether it is murder.

"*Direct abortion, that is, abortion willed as an end or as a means, always constitutes a grave moral disorder.*"

Abortion Is Immoral

John Paul II

In the following viewpoint, John Paul II, the pope of the Roman Catholic Church, contends that abortion is a particularly heinous crime because it kills an innocent human being who has yet to be born. Human life begins the moment an ovum is fertilized, he maintains, and every human being has a sacred and inviolable right to life.

As you read, consider the following questions:

1. What is the true nature of abortion, according to John Paul II?
2. Who is responsible for the death of an aborted baby, according to the pope?
3. In the author's opinion, how do some people try to justify abortion?

Excerpted from Pope John Paul II's encyclical "Evangelium Vitae," as it appeared in *Origins*, April 6, 1995.

Among all the crimes which can be committed against life, procured abortion has characteristics making it particularly serious and deplorable. The Second Vatican Council defines abortion, together with infanticide, as an "unspeakable crime."

But today in many people's consciences the perception of its gravity has become progressively obscured. The acceptance of abortion in the popular mind, in behavior and even in law itself, is a telling sign of an extremely dangerous crisis of the moral sense, which is becoming more and more incapable of distinguishing between good and evil even when the fundamental right to life is at stake. Given such a grave situation, we need now more than ever to have the courage to look the truth in the eye and to call things by their proper name, without yielding to convenient compromises or to the temptation of self-deception. In this regard the reproach of the prophet is extremely straightforward: "Woe to those who call evil good and good evil, who put darkness for light and light for darkness" (Isaiah 5:20). Especially in the case of abortion there is a widespread use of ambiguous terminology, such as *interruption of pregnancy*, which tends to hide abortion's true nature and to attenuate its seriousness in public opinion. Perhaps this linguistic phenomenon is itself a symptom of an uneasiness of conscience. But no word has the power to change the reality of things: Procured abortion is the deliberate and direct killing, by whatever means it is carried out, of a human being in the initial phase of his or her existence, extending from conception to birth.

Abortion Murders an Innocent Baby

The moral gravity of procured abortion is apparent in all its truth if we recognize that we are dealing with murder and, in particular, when we consider the specific elements involved. The one eliminated is a human being at the very beginning of life. No one more absolutely innocent could be imagined. In no way could this human being ever be considered an aggressor, much less an unjust aggressor! He or she is weak, defenseless, even to the point of lacking that minimal form of defense consisting in the poignant power of a newborn baby's cries and tears. The unborn child is totally entrusted to the protection and care of the woman carrying him or her in the womb. And yet sometimes it is precisely the mother herself who makes the decision and asks for the child to be eliminated, and who then goes about having it done.

It is true that the decision to have an abortion is often tragic and painful for the mother insofar as the decision to rid herself of the fruit of conception is not made for purely selfish reasons or out of convenience, but out of a desire to protect certain important values such as her own health or a decent standard of living for the other members of the family. Sometimes it is feared that the child to be born would live in such conditions that it would be better if the birth did not take place. Nevertheless, these reasons and others like them, however serious and tragic, can never justify the deliberate killing of an innocent human being.

Others Who Bear Responsibility

As well as the mother, there are often other people too who decide upon the death of the child in the womb. In the first place, the father of the child may be to blame, not only when he directly pressures the woman to have an abortion, but also when he indirectly encourages such a decision on her part by leaving her alone to face the problems of pregnancy: In this way the family is thus mortally wounded and profaned in its nature as a community of love and in its vocation to be the "sanctuary of life." Nor can one overlook the pressures which sometimes come from the wider family circle and from friends. Sometimes the woman is subjected to such strong pressure that she feels psychologically forced to have an abortion: Certainly in this case moral responsibility lies particularly with those who have directly or indirectly obliged her to have an abortion. Doctors and nurses are also responsible when they place at the service of death skills which were acquired for promoting life.

Abortion Is Wrong

The test of a civilized society, it seems to us, is how it treats the most vulnerable—the old and sick, the young and ignorant, the poor and disabled, the homeless and despised, the dispossessed and imprisoned. The least among us. Once upon a time there would have been no hesitation to include in such a category life in the womb. Now there is a "serious" question about whether it is human life at all. (What else could it be—an aardvark?) Once there was a folk metaphor for security—"as safe as a child in its mother's womb." At the rate of 1.6 million abortions a year in America circa 1993, surely few would make any such assumption now.

Abortion is wrong.

If abortion is not wrong, then nothing is.

Little Rock (Ark.) *Democrat Gazette*, March 11, 1993.

But responsibility likewise falls on the legislators who have promoted and approved abortion laws and, to the extent that they have a say in the matter, on the administrators of the health care centers where abortions are performed. A general and no less serious responsibility lies with those who have encouraged the spread of an attitude of sexual permissiveness and a lack of esteem for motherhood, and with those who should have ensured—but did not—effective family and social policies in support of families, especially larger families and those with particular financial and educational needs. Finally, one cannot overlook the network of complicity which reaches out to include international institutions, foundations and associations which systematically campaign for the legalization and spread of abortion in the world. In this sense abortion goes beyond the responsibility of individuals and beyond the harm done to them, and takes on a distinctly social dimension. It is a most serious wound inflicted on society and its culture by the very people who ought to be society's promoters and defenders. As I wrote in my *Letter to Families*, "We are facing an immense threat to life: not only to the life of individuals but also to that of civilization itself." We are facing what can be called a "structure of sin" which opposes human life not yet born.

The Embryo Is a Human Life

Some people try to justify abortion by claiming that the result of conception, at least up to a certain number of days, cannot yet be considered a personal human life. But in fact, the Congregation for the Doctrine of Faith's *Declaration on Procured Abortion* proclaims, "from the time that the ovum is fertilized, a life is begun which is neither that of the father nor the mother; it is rather the life of a new human being with his own growth. It would never be made human if it were not human already. This has always been clear, and . . . modern genetic science offers clear confirmation. It has demonstrated that from the first instant there is established the program of what this living being will be: a person, this individual person with his characteristic aspects already well determined. Right from fertilization the adventure of a human life begins, and each of its capacities requires time—a rather lengthy time to find its place and to be in a position to act." The Church maintains in *Donum Vitae* that even if the presence of a spiritual soul cannot be ascertained by empirical data, the results themselves of scientific research on the human embryo provide "a valuable indication for discerning by the use of reason a personal presence at the moment of the first appearance of a human life: How could a human individual not be a human person?"

Furthermore, what is at stake is so important that, from the standpoint of moral obligation, the mere probability that a human person is involved would suffice to justify an absolutely clear prohibition of any intervention aimed at killing a human embryo. . . .

Human Life Is Sacred

The texts of Sacred Scripture never address the question of deliberate abortion and so do not directly and specifically condemn it. But they show such great respect for the human being in the mother's womb that they require as a logical consequence that God's commandment "you shall not kill" be extended to the unborn child as well.

Human life is sacred and inviolable at every moment of existence, including the initial phase which precedes birth. All human beings, from their mothers' womb, belong to God who searches them and knows them, who forms them and knits them together with his own hands, who gazes on them when they are tiny shapeless embryos and already sees in them the adults of tomorrow whose days are numbered and whose vocation is even now written in the "book of life" (cf. Psalms 139:1, 13-16). There too, when they are still in their mothers' womb—as many passages of the Bible bear witness—they are the personal objects of God's loving and fatherly providence.

Christian tradition—as the declaration issued by the Congregation for the Doctrine of the Faith points out so well—is clear and unanimous from the beginning up to our own day in describing abortion as a particularly grave moral disorder. From its first contacts with the Greco-Roman world, where abortion and infanticide were widely practiced, the first Christian community, by its teaching and practice radically opposed the customs rampant in that society. Among the Greek ecclesiastical writers, Athenagoras records that Christians consider as murderesses women who have recourse to abortifacient medicines, because children, even if they are still in their mothers' womb, "are already under the protection of divine providence." Among the Latin authors, Tertullian affirms: "It is anticipated murder to prevent someone from being born; it makes little difference whether one kills a soul already born or puts it to death at birth. He who will one day be a man is a man already."

Throughout Christianity's 2,000-year history, this same doctrine has been constantly taught by the fathers of the Church and by her pastors and doctors. Even scientific and philosophical discussions about the precise moment of the infusion of the spiritual soul have never given rise to any hesitation about the moral condemnation of abortion.

The Church's Condemnations

The more recent papal magisterium has vigorously reaffirmed this common doctrine. Pius XI in particular, in his encyclical *Casti Connubii*, rejected the specious justifications of abortion. Pius XII excluded all direct abortion, i.e., every act tending directly to destroy human life in the womb "whether such de-

21

struction is intended as an end or only as a means to an end." John XXIII reaffirmed that human life is sacred because "from its very beginning it directly involves God's creative activity." The Second Vatican Council, as mentioned earlier, sternly condemned abortion: "From the moment of its conception life must be guarded with the greatest care, while abortion and infanticide are unspeakable crimes."

The Church's canonical discipline from the earliest centuries has inflicted penal sanctions on those guilty of abortion. This practice, with more or less severe penalties, has been confirmed in various periods of history. The 1917 Code of Canon Law punished abortion with excommunication. The revised canonical legislation continues this tradition when it decrees that "a person who actually procures an abortion incurs automatic (*latae sententiae*) excommunication." The excommunication affects all those who commit this crime with knowledge of the penalty attached and thus includes those accomplices without whose help the crime would not have been committed. By this reiterated sanction, the Church makes clear that abortion is a most serious and dangerous crime, thereby encouraging those who commit it to seek without delay the path of conversion. In the Church the purpose of the penalty of excommunication is to make an individual fully aware of the gravity of a certain sin and then to foster genuine conversion and repentance.

A Grave Moral Disorder

Given such unanimity in the doctrinal and disciplinary tradition of the Church, Paul VI was able to declare that this tradition is unchanged and unchangeable. Therefore, by the authority which Christ conferred upon Peter and his successors, in communion with the bishops—who on various occasions have condemned abortion and who in the aforementioned consultation, albeit dispersed throughout the world, have shown unanimous agreement concerning this doctrine—*I declare that direct abortion, that is, abortion willed as an end or as a means, always constitutes a grave moral disorder*, since it is the deliberate killing of an innocent human being. This doctrine is based upon the natural law and upon the written word of God, is transmitted by the Church's tradition and taught by the ordinary and universal magisterium.

No circumstance, no purpose, no law whatsoever can ever make licit an act which is intrinsically illicit, since it is contrary to the law of God which is written in every human heart, knowable by reason itself and proclaimed by the Church.

"Under some conditions, choosing to give birth may be socially dysfunctional, morally irresponsible or even cruel."

Abortion Is Sometimes a Moral Choice

Jerry Z. Muller

In the following viewpoint, Jerry Z. Muller argues that abortion can be a moral choice when the fetus has a birth defect or when the pregnancy is unwanted. Children who are born out of wedlock to women who are not prepared to raise a child are more likely to be unable to function in society and to become violent or criminals, Muller asserts. When abortion is an available option, he maintains, most children who are born will be healthy and wanted. Muller is a history professor at Catholic University of America in Washington, D.C.

As you read, consider the following questions:

1. What is the ultimate aim of the right-to-life movement, in Muller's opinion?
2. According to the author, how many abortions are performed on married and unmarried women?
3. What are the three factions in the abortion debate, according to Muller?

Jerry Z. Muller, "The Conservative Case for Abortion," *New Republic*, August 21 & 28, 1995. Reprinted by permission of the *New Republic*; ©1995, The New Republic, Inc.

In contemporary American political debate, struggles over abortion are usually treated as conflicts between rival interpretations of individual rights. Those who favor abortion most often invoke the "right to choose" of the woman who has conceived the fetus. Those who oppose abortion focus on the "right to life" of the fetus. But there is a third position that is largely overlooked. Essentially conservative and "pro-family," it favors abortion as the right choice to promote healthy family life under certain circumstances.

Birth Is Not Always the Right Choice

This argument, which emphasizes the social function of the family over the rights of the individual, begins with the assumption that the possibility of choice matters less than the choices made. It argues that the choice to give birth to a child isn't always the right one. In fact, under some conditions, choosing to give birth may be socially dysfunctional, morally irresponsible or even cruel: inimical to the forces of stability and bourgeois responsibility conservatives cherish.

Supporters of middle-class family values may agree with many Christian Coalition positions. They may advocate raising the income-tax deduction for dependent children, question the legitimation of homosexuality and condemn violence and sex in the cultural marketplace. But the right-to-life position undermines their fundamentally conservative effort to strengthen purposeful families. For the right-to-life position requires massive government intrusion into the most intimate of realms, removes decisions about whether to bear children from those who are to raise them and threatens what many conservatives regard as the most significant mediating institution in modern capitalist society, the family. The success of the right-to-life position would lead almost inevitably to an increase in the number of children born into socially dysfunctional settings.

The prime obstacle to the right-to-life movement is not feminism. It is the millions of more or less conservative middle-class parents who know that, if their teenage daughter were to become pregnant, they would advise her to get an abortion rather than marry out of necessity or go through the trauma of giving birth and then placing the child up for adoption. Many people—young, unmarried, pregnant women loath to bring a child into a family-less environment; parents of a fetus known to be afflicted by a disease such as Tay-Sachs that will make its life painful and short; parents whose children are likely to be born with severe genetic defects, who know that the birth of the fetus will mean pain for them and for their other children—all choose abortion, not because they fetishize choice but because they value the family. Many couples who know that their offspring will be at risk for genetic diseases and other birth defects owe their actual families to abortion: were it not for the possibility of detecting these diseases in utero and of aborting stricken fetuses, such couples would not risk having children at all.

The Right-to-Life Movement's Aim

The right-to-life movement regards human "life" as a good—a claim most of us are broadly inclined to accept. But the right-to-life movement goes further. It regards *all* human life as a good, regardless of the mental, emotional or intellectual capacities of the individual. To right-to-lifers, keeping alive anencephalic infants (children missing all or most of their brains) is a moral imperative. The right-to-life movement regards every degree of human life as equal to the most complete development of human life: that is why the moral status of a fetus two weeks into its development is the same as that of children and adults.

For the right-to-life movement, then, human life is not only a good, it is the highest good, and it is always the highest good. The movement's strategic aim is to extend state power to preserve and protect every fetus that is conceived, regardless of the circumstances under which it is conceived, regardless of the condition of the fetus and regardless of the will of the fetus's parents.

The Moral Choice

Even though it kills human life, abortion is, in fact, the moral choice to make when would-be mothers ascertain that their present circumstances do not enable them to raise a would-be child responsibly. Contrary to popular accusation, it is not the decision to abort but the decision to have a child that is treated with insufficient gravity in our society.

Kathleen Quinn, *Mother Jones*, November/December 1993.

The right-to-life movement has done our society a service by insisting upon the humanity and moral worth of the unborn child. But opponents of abortion have turned a legitimate moral concern into a moral absolute. They have made biological life not one good to be fought for, but the only good, to which all others must be subordinated. For this reason, anti-abortion activists insist that abortion be forbidden in cases of rape or incest: to suggest there are moral considerations other than those of the life of the fetus is to question the fundamental premises of the right-to-life movement.

One of those considerations is the creation and preservation of families. The pro-life movement is at odds with the assumptions of middle-class family formation. These families believe that the bearing and rearing of children is not an inexorable fate but a voluntary vocation, and that, like any other vocation, it is to be pursued methodically using the most effective means available. Such a conception of the family includes planning when children are to be born and how many are to be born. It seeks to increase the chances of successfully socializing and educating children in order to help them find fulfilling work and spiritual lives. The number of children is kept low in part because the amount of parental time and resources devoted to raising them is expected to be high.

This depiction of the middle-class family as a vocation borrows from the characterization of economic activity as a vocation in Max Weber's *The Protestant Ethic and the Spirit of Capitalism*. Weber argued that a key element in the rise of capitalism was a notion of economic activity as purposeful. This notion motivated those most active in capitalist economic activity, providing an alternative to traditional, fatalistic conceptions of economic life. Just as older patterns of economic traditionalism and fatalism persist within advanced industrial societies, fatalistic conceptions of family life remain as well, in which families are not consciously "made" but "happen" because fate has so decreed.

The Middle-Class Family

Declining fertility is universal among advanced industrial societies. Beginning in the European bourgeois family, fertility was consciously curtailed by contraception or abortion when the desired and limited number of children was reached. By the late nineteenth century, marriage in Europe was increasingly postponed until a decade or more after puberty, and one or another form of contraception allowed greater control over the timing and spacing of births.

The technological repertoire of today's family planning includes abortion to prevent out-of-wedlock childbirth, artificial contraception within marriage and voluntary sterilization when families have reached their desired size. This activist conception of family formation also suggests that artificial reproductive technology should be used to reverse infertility. Prenatal screening is part of the package: potential children known to carry debilitating diseases may be aborted to make possible the birth of children more likely to grow into healthy, productive adulthood. Given the assumptions of middle-class family formation, ignoring such technological possibilities can even be regarded as a form of child neglect.

This middle-class vision of the family is linked to other elements of modern life. It is a conception that those who seek to conserve modern society ought to fortify rather than undermine. It is under attack from many quarters, including the individualism and hedonism of much of our popular and elite culture and the emphasis on career advancement among both men and women. But it is also threatened from another direction by the right-to-life movement.

Family Ideals

The struggle between the ideals of middle-class family formation and more fatalistic conceptions of family life is in part a struggle between groups in our society with divergent conceptions of rational, purposeful behavior. Members of the upper middle class are usually either the product of families with a rational, purposeful, planned view of domestic life or have adopted such behavior on their own. It is no coincidence that the Evangelical Protestant denominations that most vociferously oppose abortion draw disproportionately from the lower middle and working classes, emphasize faith as the antidote to fate and stress redemption through divine grace rather than through a lifetime of purposeful activity.

The ideology of middle-class family formation maintains that families are not just another lifestyle option but an essential part of a modern society. Illegitimacy is stigmatized because it is socially dysfunctional. Conservatives have long assumed that government should promote those social norms that encourage the creation of decent men and women and discourage those that experience has shown to be harmful. This logic lies at the heart of conservative debates on public policy, including recent proposals to reform welfare to discourage out-of-wedlock births.

The right-to-life movement stands as a barrier to such reform. The removal of government subsidies for the bearing of out-of-wedlock children, it is said, will create an incentive for pregnant teenagers and other pregnant unmarried women to resort more frequently to abortion. Though the claim is most often articulated by pro-life opponents of welfare reform, it is also an unarticulated premise of many who favor the elimination of welfare payments to unwed mothers.

The Importance of Committed Parents

Is it more important to minimize abortion or to minimize the birth of children to women who are unprepared to provide the familial structure needed for children to become stable and responsible adults? A growing consensus holds that unsocialized children are at the heart of our social deterioration, not only because they are more likely to engage in violent and criminal activity, but because they lack the discipline needed to learn in school and to function in the workplace. The socializing influ-

27

ence of the family—comprising husbands and wives in ongoing union and with a commitment to child-rearing—appears to be an essential element of any solution. If these assumptions are correct, as conservatives and many liberals now believe, the trade-off is more biological lives at the cost of more unsocialized children—making people versus making people moral.

Humanness Is Not Enough

Yes, we can say, the foetus is a living human being, but that alone is not sufficient to show that it is wrong to end its life. After all, why—in the absence of religious beliefs about being made in the image of God, or having an immortal soul—should mere membership of the species *Homo sapiens* be crucial to whether the life of a being may or may not be taken? Surely what is important is the capacities or characteristics that a being has. It is doubtful if a foetus becomes conscious until quite late in pregnancy, well after the time at which abortions are usually performed; and even the presence of consciousness would only put a foetus at a level comparable to a rather simple non-human animal—not that of a dog, let alone a chimpanzee. If on the other hand it is self-awareness, rather than mere consciousness, that grounds a right to life, that does not arise in a human being until some time after birth.

Peter Singer, *Spectator*, September 16, 1995.

Opposition to the elimination of welfare payments for out-of-wedlock children comes from two quarters: the pro-choice movement and the right-to-life movement. The former condemns "welfare caps" because they reduce the choices facing women, and all choices are to be protected. In the words of liberal feminist Iris Young, "A liberal society that claims to respect the autonomy of all its citizens equally should affirm the freedom of all citizens to bear and rear children, whether they are married or not, whether they have high incomes or not." For the right-to-life movement, of course, no fact about the potentially miserable outcome of the fetus's birth affects the imperative that it be born. Beginning from different commitments, therefore, feminists and pro-lifers converge in rejecting the conservative assumption that the troubling social effects of out-of-wedlock births justify government attempts to limit them.

Out-of-Wedlock Births

The current right-to-life strategy calls for "chipping away" at the liberal abortion culture to "save" as many babies as possible under the political circumstances. Because pro-lifers can have the greatest impact on legislation affecting the poor, the socially marginal and those dependent on governmental funding for medical procedures, among their first targets have been, for example, Medicaid recipients. As a result, the success of the pro-life movement is now measured in the lives of poor children born out of wedlock. Most abortions in the U.S. occur to avoid the birth of children out of wedlock. Of the roughly 1.5 million abortions in 1991, only 271,000 were performed upon married women. Among married women, there were eight abortions for every ninety births; among unmarried women, there were forty-eight abortions for every forty-five births. All else being equal, then, eliminating the possibility of abortion would hike the number of out-of-wedlock births from its already disastrous level of 30 percent to 49 percent.

Indeed, the anti-abortion movement may already have helped increase the number of children born out of wedlock. The percentage of out-of-wedlock births in the United States rose from 18.4 percent in 1980 to 30.1 percent f all births in 1992, according to recent reports from the National Center for Health Statistics. During the same period, the proportion of non-marital pregnancies ending in abortion declined, from 60 percent in 1980 to 46 percent in 1991, and the abortion rate among unmarried women fell by 12 percent. Thirty percent of these mothers were teenagers. The statistics on all potential mothers aged 15 to 17, those least able to care adequately for their children, are more alarming still. In the years from 1986 to 1991 the pregnancy rate for this group rose by 7 percent, but the abortion rate dropped by 19 percent, so that the rate of out-of-wedlock births among these very young mothers increased by 27 percent. This trend toward out-of-wedlock births rather than abortion may be due either to the increased difficulty of obtaining abortions or to increased preference for carrying babies to term. Either way, it marks a partial victory for the pro-life movement.

Late-Term Abortions

The second thrust of the current right-to-life strategy is the prohibition of abortion late in pregnancy, on the plausible assumption that even those with doubts about prohibiting abortion entirely regard the fetus as subject to ever greater respect as it develops. Here, too, the effect is tragic. Late-term abortions are rare, and, when they do occur, it is frequently because the parents have discovered late that their prospective child suffers from a serious birth defect or malformation. Yet it is these fetuses whom the pro-life movement now aims to "save." A bill before the 104th Congress tries to force women to give birth to such babies. Titled the Partial-Birth Abortion Ban Act by its sponsors, it would be better dubbed the Cruelty to Families Act.

[The bill passed in both houses of Congress in late 1995 and was vetoed by Bill Clinton in April 1996.]

The public is genuinely ambivalent on the question of abortion. It adheres to the tenets of middle-class family life, yet without hearing those tenets articulated. To focus on the conflict between the right-to-life movement and middle-class family values is to call into question the terms in which the abortion debate is usually cast in our political culture. The abortion struggle should be understood as a three-way debate: among liberals, who believe that to let each of us do as we like will work out for the best; pro-lifers, who cling to one ultimate good at the expense of all others; and those committed to conserving middle-class families, sometimes at the expense of "choice," sometimes at the expense of "life." The third group lays best claim to the title "conservative."

"'Kill' . . . is a perfectly legitimate term to describe what abortion actually does to the unborn child."

Abortion Is Murder

William Brennan

Every year in the United States 1.5 million abortions are performed. This statistic has been justly used to portray abortion as a modern-day Holocaust, contends William Brennan in the following viewpoint. Each abortion kills an unborn child, he maintains. Just as the Jewish Holocaust in Nazi Germany was legal but morally wrong, Brennan argues, abortions are legal but not moral. Brennan is a social services professor at St. Louis University and the author of *Dehumanizing the Vulnerable: When Word Games Take Lives* and *When Life and Choice Collide*.

As you read, consider the following questions:

1. How does the number of abortions performed compare with the number of Jews killed during the Holocaust, according to Brennan?
2. In the author's opinion, what are some of the ways in which abortions are similar to the Holocaust?
3. What is the role of the American media in the abortion debate, and what should it be, in Brennan's view?

William Brennan, "What the Holocaust and Abortion Have in Common," *New Oxford Review*, November 1995. This article was adapted from the original, which appeared in *When Life and Choice Collide: Essays on Rhetoric and Abortion*, vol. 1, *To Set the Dawn Free*, edited by David Mall (Libertyville, IL: Kairos Books, 1994), pp. 189–202. Reprinted by permission.

On March 14, 1984, the *New York Times* stooped very low in its relentless campaign to discredit anyone who dares challenge the contemporary abortion juggernaut. The target of the *Times'* wrath was New York Archbishop John J. O'Connor because he linked abortion with the Nazi Holocaust. For this, O'Connor was subjected to a severe tongue-lashing and thrust into that time-worn caricature of a shadowy religious zealot bent on imposing his narrow sectarian morality on everyone else. An insidious inference was also made that O'Connor's remarks smacked of anti-Semitism.

O'Connor stood by his analogy, refused to be intimidated by the bullying tactics of the mega-press, and rightly responded with outrage at the blatantly false and offensive insinuations drawn. Letters to the *Times* reflected considerable support for the bishop (now cardinal). Former U.S. Supreme Court Justice Arthur Goldberg wrote: "Any inference in your editorial that Bishop O'Connor in any way minimized the tragedy of the Holocaust is . . . entirely without foundation and constitutes an unwarranted aspersion on . . . [his record of] total abhorrence of anti-Semitism in any form."

Abortion Is a Modern-Day Holocaust

O'Connor is not the only prominent individual to portray abortion as a modern-day Holocaust. Congressman Henry Hyde, former U.S. Surgeon General C. Everett Koop, and Malcolm Muggeridge are among the notables who have publicly compared abortion to the Nazi war against the Jews. In his article, "Abortion and the Conscience of the Nation," President Ronald Reagan quoted a passage from *The Abortion Holocaust: Today's Final Solution* which underscores a basic principle related to both abortion and the Nazi Holocaust: "The cultural environment for a human holocaust is present whenever any society can be misled into defining individuals as less than human and therefore devoid of value and respect."

It was in a television interview on WNBC's "Newsforum" (March 11, 1984) that O'Connor had highlighted a series of parallels between abortion and the Nazi Holocaust. He emphasized that "I always compare the killing of 4,000 babies a day in the United States, unborn babies, to the Holocaust."

In this statement he violated two sacrosanct principles of abortionspeak: Never call abortion "killing" and never refer to the victims of abortion as "unborn babies." In today's abortion culture, where destructive activities have been technologically and semantically transformed into minor medical procedures, O'Connor's style of expression is considered downright tasteless, much too graphic, and a grave threat to the very credibility of the abortion establishment and the media elite which play such an indispensable role in disseminating proabortion rhetoric.

Despite the pervasive efforts to malign anyone who employs the word "kill" when referring to abortion, this is a perfectly legitimate term to describe what abortion actually does to the unborn child. When the abortionist invades the sanctuary of the womb, the passenger within is by all scientific criteria alive, growing, and developing. After the abortionist accomplishes his lethal task, the intrauterine victim is definitely no longer alive, and therefore dead. And it is the abortion procedure that brought about this death.

To call abortion anything less than killing is, as has been so cogently pointed out by former abortion clinic director Dr. Bernard Nathanson, "the crassest kind of moral evasiveness."

There are some other remarkably revealing insights into the essence of abortion that provide a solid factual foundation for the comparisons stressed by O'Connor. As far back as 1859, the American Medical Association House of Delegates, in a historic policy statement against abortion, referred to abortion as "the slaughter of countless children" and "unwarrantable destruction of human life." In 1871 the AMA reiterated its opposition to abortion in the strongest terms, calling it "the wholesale destruction of unborn infants." Periodically, even some contemporary abortionists and abortion supporters acknowledge the true nature of abortion. Fetal research advocates Drs. Willard Gaylin and Marc Lappe describe abortion procedures as "unimaginable acts of violence." According to veteran abortionist Dr. Warren Hern, D and E [dilation and evacuation] abortion is "an act of destruction."

Not only did O'Connor call abortion what it is, he also pointed out that the killing of the unborn is comparable in scope to the Nazi extermination of Jews. The number of unborn lives extinguished by abortion is staggering: 4,000 on a daily basis, over 1.6 million annually, and over 30 million in the 20 years after the U.S. Supreme Court rendered its proabortion decision in 1973. On a worldwide annual basis the abortion toll has reached astronomical proportions: 50 to 60 million. And there is no letup in sight! During the 12 years of the Third Reich, the Nazis did away with six million Jews, 275,000 German handicapped, a quarter million Gypsies, and untold numbers of unborn children in the occupied Eastern territories.

Disposing of the Bodies

O'Connor also focused on the strikingly similar methods employed to get rid of past and present victims defined as problems: "Now Hitler tried to solve a problem, the Jewish question. So kill them, shove them in the ovens, burn them. Well, we claim that unborn babies are a problem, so kill them. To me it really is precisely the same."

Burning in crematory ovens and huge ditches constituted the predominant means of body disposal in the Nazi killing centers. Huge numbers of aborted bodies today are likewise disposed of by burning in hospital furnaces or city incinerators.

At the Treblinka death camp a major controversy erupted over whether the bodies of victims should be buried or burned. Odilio Globocnik, an SS officer consumed with Nazi ideals, defended burying the bodies and placing bronze plaques over the mass graves with the inscription: "It was we, we who had the courage to achieve this gigantic task." Dr. Herbert Linden, a realist, countered with the observation: "But would it not be better to burn the bodies instead of burying them? A future generation might think differently of these matters." Reality won out over idealism and the order was given to burn all bodies, including those previously buried.

Reprinted by permission of Chuck Asay and Creators Syndicate.

A similar debate raged over what to do with more than 16,000 aborted babies discovered in a huge metal storage container outside of Los Angeles in 1982. Prolife groups were in favor of at least according these victims the dignity of a Christian burial. The American Civil Liberties Union, a staunch proponent of burning the bodies, conjured up that all too predictable concoction—violation of separation of church and state—to block the burial.

One cannot help but conclude that the ACLU, like the Nazi realists, favors burning not because of legal principles or ideals, but because this particular method of disposal permanently removes all telltale traces of mass destruction. Burial, especially Christian burial, is doubly threatening: Not only does it bestow upon the victims a transcendent value intolerable to civil libertarians, it also draws attention to a disturbing truth which abortionists would prefer to keep hidden from public view—the existence of actual human bodies.

Code Words for Killing

Nazi perpetrators and contemporary abortionists share another important attribute: a persistent habit of calling what has been done to their respective victims something other than killing.

Nazi semanticists avoided the word "kill" like a plague, and manufactured an unprecedented list of code words, slogans, and euphemisms to cover up their destructive actions. According to the Nazi lexicon, people were simply "removed" from ghettoes and "evacuated" to "the East" for "resettlement," "special treatment," or "rehabilitation" in the "bathhouses" and "wash and disinfectant rooms" of "labor," "concentration," or "resettlement" camps.

Abortion linguists are equally averse to using any unpleasant terms, especially "kill," when referring to their deadly procedures. They too have created an extensive vocabulary of euphemisms and abstract phrases to conceal horrendous realities. In the sugar-coated abortion versions, "products" or "contents" are merely "removed" or "evacuated" from the womb in the antiseptic settings of "reproductive health centers," "clinics," or "preterm institutes."

Much of the inoffensive language fabricated by past and present perpetrators has taken on a strong medical flavor. A study of former death camp doctors conducted by American psychiatrist Robert Jay Lifton revealed that medical involvement in the Holocaust was projected not as killing, but as a "medical operation." This is exactly how abortion doctors justify their assaults on the unborn: as "medical procedures" or "minor medical operations." At the Nazis' Hadamar euthanasia hospital, patients about to be killed by lethal injections were told that the substances administered were for "treatment of their lung disease." Dr. Willard Cates presented a paper before a meeting of Planned Parenthood Physicians entitled: "Abortion as a Treatment for Unwanted Pregnancy: The Number Two Sexually Transmitted 'Disease.'"

These malignant metaphors are manifestations of a process best characterized as the medicalization of destruction. As such, they symbolize the most radical of transformations: the redefinition of killing as a type of medical treatment, and the reconceptualization of the victims as disease entities.

The Right to Choose to Kill

For those politicians who maintain that "I personally am opposed to abortion, but, after all, we must have a choice," O'Connor made a pertinent observation: "You show me the politician who is prepared to say, 'I personally am opposed to . . . killing Blacks or Jewish people . . . but we have to have a choice.' That's . . . sheer absurdity."

Here O'Connor confronted the most sacred cow of abortion rhetoric: "choice" or "the right to choose." Those who rely on these slogans rarely specify the right to choose what for whom. Beneath this democratic facade lurks an especially reprehensible form of oppression: the right to choose to kill innocent human beings who cannot defend themselves.

The Nazi medics utilized almost identical designations—"selection," or they were "selected"—to cover up death camp atrocities. They never elaborated upon the true nature of their selections. Such seductive semantics were intended to obscure a particularly deplorable type of tyranny, namely, the right to select helpless victims for mass extermination.

A Barbaric Homicide

In the emerging, post-Christian new world order, human beings increasingly are viewed as products to be created (naturally and unnaturally), bought, sold, cannibalized for organs and destroyed at the whim and will of greedy businesses and ghoulish practitioners. This is the worst kind of barbarism.

Human life begins at the instant of fertilization/conception. The willful taking of innocent human life by any means constitutes homicide and is a great moral and social evil. Society must not sanction the taking of any single innocent human life or else all human life will thereby be devalued.

Human Life International Position Statement

"Proselection" and "prochoice" semantics have proven to be enormously effective weapons in helping facilitate past and contemporary holocausts. Toward the latter part of July 1944, women who contracted scarlet fever were gassed to death at Auschwitz. This destruction process was classified as "a selection." In June 1981 doctors at New York's Mount Sinai Hospital announced they had pierced the heart and extracted half of the blood from an unwanted unborn twin afflicted with Down's syndrome. *Newsweek* dubbed this destructive procedure "a choice in the womb." Thus, Nazi doctors had "the right to select" who perished in gas chambers, just as today's abortion doctors in collaboration with women insist on "the right to choose" who will expire in abortion chambers.

Dehumanizing the Victims

One other significant feature common to both Nazi and abortion rhetoric is the pervasive pattern of dehumanizing victims through the imposition of derogatory labels. A study of the disparaging language inevitably leads to the conclusion that abortionists and their most ardent supporters deny the humanity of the unborn as vociferously as the Nazis denied the humanity of the Jews.

Situation ethics professor Joseph Fletcher has frequently referred to the unborn, especially if afflicted with a handicap, as "subhuman life in utero." Amitai Etzioni, who calls himself a "communitarian," has favored the development of "procedures and criteria for determining who and what shall live or die and which fetuses are tissue and which are human." He has defined the unborn during the first four and one-half months of pregnancy as "subhuman and relatively close to a piece of tissue."

Paradoxically, Etzioni, a Jew, resorts to the same terminology against the unborn as the Nazis used against his ancestors. His preoccupation with such demeaning categories as "subhuman" bears an alarming resemblance to the Nazi approach to determining who would survive and who would not. On many an occasion Adolf Hitler asserted that "Jews are not human." University of Strasbourg anatomy professor Dr. August Hirt, whose research consisted of trying to demonstrate the inferiority of the Jewish race through an examination of skulls severed from gas chamber victims, referred to his subjects as "subhumanity."

The images of Jews as "nonhuman" and "subhuman" did not originate with Hitler and his cohorts. One of the most significant but least publicized facts is that many of these depersonalized perceptions emanated from liberal intellectual circles. Jacob Katz in *From Prejudice to Destruction* and Alfred Low in *Jews in the Eyes of the Germans* indicate that numerous demeaning stereotypes foisted on Jews were the handiwork of German intellectuals, many of whom possessed impeccable liberal credentials. As early as 1819 Christoph Heinrich Pfaff, described in Katz's book as "an individual of high intellectual standards and genuine liberal convictions," compared Jews to "a rapidly growing parasitic plant that winds round the still healthy tree to suck up the life juice until the trunk, emaciated and eaten up from within, falls moldering into decay."

Similarly, the members of today's American liberal community are among the most steadfast promoters of subhuman semantics directed against the unborn. Liberals repeatedly proclaim how much they care about an ever burgeoning list of oppressed groups, including blacks, women, the poor, homosexuals, and endangered animals. At the same time they remain completely oblivious to the existence, let alone plight, of the most thoroughly oppressed minority group in contemporary society: unborn children. In a style strikingly reminiscent of the German anti-Semitic liberal Pfaff, today's radical feminists frequently reduce the unborn to "a parasite" or "a parasite within the mother's body."

Killing at the level of a holocaust is enhanced enormously when the derogatory mentality toward the victims becomes embedded in the legal structure. At first the designation "nonperson," along with "nonhuman," "subhuman," and "parasite," functions to dehumanize those so labeled. Later the term "nonperson" is transformed into a legal construct which has the effect of stripping away rights from the victims and elevating their destruction to the exalted level of legality. In *The Dual State: A Contribution to the Study of German Dictatorship*, legal scholar Ernst Fraenkel noted that the German Supreme Court in 1936 "refused to recognize Jews living in Germany as 'persons' in the legal sense." In 1973 the U.S. Supreme Court declared that "the word 'person,' as used in the Fourteenth Amendment, does not include the unborn."

Political scientist Hannah Arendt considered the "nonperson" concept a crucial cornerstone of the victimization process intrinsic to totalitarian governments. In *The Origins of Totalitarianism*, she indicates that the hallmark of a totalitarian state, whether Communist or fascist, is to declare those deemed stateless and expendable as "legal nonpersons." According to this criterion, the U.S. qualifies as a totalitarian society because unborn children, chiefly through the device of "legal nonpersonhood," have been rendered stateless and outside the law's protection, whereby doctors can inflict unimaginable acts of violence on a massive scale with full-fledged legal support.

A Legal Matter

Once a practice is legalized, even one so repulsive as large-scale killing, it is endowed with immense respectability. Then the law itself becomes a prime justification for participation in destructive activities. And the practitioners of malevolent deeds can be expected to invoke the law relentlessly.

"What is legal is moral" is an astoundingly effective slogan utilized to vindicate all types of atrocities. At the Nuremberg Doctors' Trial in 1947, defendant Walter Schmidt projected responsibility for the Nazi Holocaust onto the legal system. "The jurists in Berlin," he testified, "told us that this was a legal matter . . . quite legal." Today's abortionists defend themselves in the same manner.

The American media elite would do well to start probing the corruption of language and thought that masks the medical execution of millions inside the womb. For too long the watchdogs of public perception in the mainstream secular media have functioned as agents of destruction-inducing propaganda by accepting at face value the euphemistic and dehumanizing rhetoric circulated by the abortion establishment. Today's gatekeepers of public information need to abandon their selective, schizophrenic brand of reporting morality and start covering the contemporary medical war on the unwanted unborn at least as directly and graphically as they have covered the Vietnam War, the horrors of capital punishment, and the slaughter of seals, dolphins, whales, and eagles.

=====

"Calling abortion 'murder' doesn't make it murder. We are hearing someone's value judgment placed on what others do."

=====

Abortion Is Not Murder

Don Sloan

In the following viewpoint, obstetrician and gynecologist Don Sloan argues that although an abortion destroys an embryo, it is not murder. The embryo or fetus is not a separate human life because it is not able to live outside the woman's body, he maintains. Moreover, people who would forbid abortions except in the case of rape or incest are not consistent in their belief that abortion is always murder, Sloan contends.

As you read, consider the following questions:

1. In Sloan's opinion, when does a fetus become a person?
2. Why is the right to life not absolute, according to the author?
3. What is the one thing that would stop most abortions, according to C. Everett Koop, as quoted by Sloan?

From *Abortion: A Doctor's Perspective, a Woman's Dilemma* by Don Sloan, M.D., with Paula Hartz. Copyright ©1992 by Don Sloan and Paula Hartz. Used by permission of Donald I. Fine, an imprint of Penguin Books USA Inc.

"Uncle Don, could I talk to you?"

My niece Jessica cornered me at a Thanksgiving Day family affair. My three sisters and I were all born within two weeks of that last Thursday in November, so it was a special celebration in the Sloan household. I always tried to make sure I was there. From the look in Jessica's eyes, it appeared that I was about to be called on to perform some avuncular duties. I hoped I was up to the task.

"Sure, Jess. What's up?"

"Did Mom say anything to you about the frog thing?"

"No. What 'frog thing'?"

"I have to, you know, dissect a frog? For biology lab. And—well, the frog's alive. I mean, can't I learn the same stuff from a book? It's *alive*. Why do I have to kill it? It's all so gross."

I had never known Jessica that well, but we weren't strangers, either. I thought if there were anything startling about her, I would have known it. Her devotion to the preservation of life had never come up before—yet it had apparently been there all along.

"What happens if you don't dissect the frog?" I asked her.

"I guess I flunk. Maybe not *flunk*, but even if I ace the written final, a third of my grade is lab, and I'll get a big fat zero in that." Jessica sighed. "For sure, it's going to mess up my average. If I really flunk, I won't have enough credits to graduate. It's a required course. Mom and Dad will go bananas. They're already partway there. Especially Dad. You know him." She shrugged. "But it's *my* frog, isn't it?"

Fetuses Versus Newborns

"You do abortions on pregnant women, don't you?" Jessica asked, as if there were some other kind.

The question took me by surprise. I also hadn't known Jessica was aware of what I did. High school is a whole other place from when I went there. The sexual revolution, explicit language, advertising, rated movies, MTV—all the media push kids into growing up fast now, even faster than they want to, maybe. Jessica obviously knew about abortion, knew it was controversial. And she had made a connection. It brought me up short. I hadn't tied the two together myself. Was abortion the same as "killing frogs"?

"Yes, Jessica, I do abortions. It's an important part of my work."

"How can you do that? I don't even want to kill a frog. Isn't that like killing babies?"

"No. It's not." I answered her abruptly. I wanted her to make her point.

There are some pundits who argue that if we are allowed to kill fetuses, we should be able to kill newborns too. After all, there's not much difference between a newborn and a fetus, and if you can destroy one, why not the other?

But to me, it's a specious argument. . . .

There are some who argue that if we can justify destroying embryos because they're not "like us"—like human adults—then we might as well kill newborns, because they're more like fetuses than they are like grown people. But rationally most people know there's a difference. When does a fetus become a person? There's no clear dividing line. When does a stream become a river? When does a child become an adult? We may not be able to put an exact date on it, but we can tell the difference. . . .

An Embryo Is Not a Baby

"How does a woman make up her mind?" Jessica asked earnestly. "If the woman doesn't want a baby, and it's going to mess up her life, I know, but still, it's a *baby*. Not right then—later on, it'll be a baby, right?"

"Yes, it'll be a baby. What kind and how healthy, I don't know. But that's irrelevant. That's just what the woman doesn't want. Jessica, at the time when we do most abortions, it's not a baby. It's an embryo or a tiny fetus that has an existence only inside the woman's body."

"But the baby—the embryo—it dies, right?"

"It can't live outside the uterus. It gets everything from the mother's body. It's living tissue of sorts. So, yes, in one sense, it dies. But it was never viable—able to live on its own." I kept wondering how much of this Jessica was understanding.

"You say it's not a baby—it's an embryo or something. But if it'll be a baby someday, what's the difference?"

"Think about acorns and oak trees. The acorn is the fertilized egg of the oak. That doesn't make it an oak tree, right? And even after it starts to grow, you don't call it a tree. You call it an acorn that's sprouted or a seedling. It's a potential tree, but it's not a tree yet. Something very special is going to happen to that growth to make it into what we know is a tree because it's able to do what a tree does. There's no clear moment when it becomes a tree, but that doesn't mean you can't tell when it's a tree and when it's not. It's the same with fetal growth."

"That sounds too simple—and weird. People aren't oak trees. You make it sound like fetuses aren't human life."

To Jessica, "weird" was an all-encompassing term. You had to interpret what she intended it to mean.

"I wouldn't deny that they're human tissue. Of course they are, as I said. And while they're attached to the woman, that tissue is alive. But they're not independent life, and they're not people as we know them. They don't have brain waves and sensitivity to pain yet."

"Don't they jump if you poke them?"

"Yes, but that doesn't mean they're feeling pain. Anything jumps if it's poked—an amoeba, an earthworm. Or your frog."

"Oh, gosh, yes. My frog. I almost forgot about that. . . . It's not hurting anybody. Why should I hurt it? Doesn't it have a right to be alive?"

"Generally speaking, no. Only people have rights—or can have them taken away."

A Far-Fetched Speculation

I wonder if people realize how big a fertilized ovum is. Half an inch? A quarter-inch? It is less than the thickness of one of your hairs! That is not a "baby." Many zygotes or embryos spontaneously abort and over 90% of deliberate abortions happen in the first trimester when the embryo is less than two inches long.

Gruesome photos of full-grown, near-term fetuses show the dire exception and extreme rarity, not the rule. Such images are deliberately deceptive and emotionally misleading. Yet the pro-life movement persists in pretending that aborting a zygote or an embryo is the same as "killing a baby." A small mass of developing cells is not a baby; it hasn't the neural mass, organization or experience to have much sentience. For early pregnancy, when most abortions occur, supposing otherwise is far-fetched speculation.

Byron Bradley Carrier, *Human Quest*, September/October 1993.

The phrase "right to life" sounds good, but courts have traditionally found that the right to life is not absolute—especially where the rights of others are concerned. Not long ago, the father of a twelve-year-old boy with leukemia sued the mother of his three-year-old twins, the product of a liaison, to allow them to be tested as possible bone-marrow donors. The older boy's only hope was a bone-marrow transplant, and his half siblings represented his best chance for life.

The mother refused on the grounds that testing the twins was intrusive and a violation of their bodily integrity. She argued that it might be frightening or even harmful to them.

The court found for the mother. She could not be compelled to allow her children to be tested. Their half brother did not get the bone-marrow transplant, and he died.

The rights of the two sides collided. You might argue that children have become bone-marrow donors for their siblings on any number of occasions and no harm came of it; you might argue that the twins' mother was morally obligated to try to save the life of their half brother; you might argue that a twelve-year-old boy deserves a chance at life even if somebody else's rights have to be violated just a little. But the fact is that one person cannot be forced to use his or her body to save another, no matter what.

At least not so far.

Abortion Is Not Murder

Jessica sighed. "The thing is, I don't want to kill the frog, but I don't really want to give up graduation and stuff for a frog, either. I'm stuck. I've got two choices, and they're both bad. Either I murder my frog, or I flunk my course." There was no gray area for Jessica at this point.

"Even if you kill the frog, Jess, it wouldn't be murder."

"Murder, kill. What's the difference? Isn't it wrong, all the same?"

"'Wrong' is a value judgment. Lots of things that are wrong to some are not to others, and they're not against the law. It would be wrong, I think, to torture the frog, but it's not a crime. *Murder* is a loaded word. It makes things sound a lot worse than they are. You're putting a value judgment on your actions when you use such terms."

"A lot of people call abortion murder, don't they?"

Is abortion murder? All killing isn't murder. A cop shoots a teenager who "appeared to be going for a gun," and we call it "justifiable homicide"—a tragedy for all concerned, but not murder if the gun was there and the cop was acting in the line of duty. And then there's war. In theory, soldiers shoot only at each other. But in practice, lots and lots of other folks get killed. We drop bombs where there are noncombatants—women and children and old people—and when they die, we call it not murder but "collateral damage." Our soldiers get killed by "friendly fire"—often by people who aimed directly at them. Is that murder? All killing like that, to me, is morally wrong. But murder?

Calling abortion "murder" doesn't make it murder. We are hearing someone's value judgment placed on what others do. . . .

Exceptions to the "Right to Life"

Self-defense isn't considered murder; in our culture, there is a right to kill in self-defense. There are people who try to make the case that abortion is a kind of self-defense: The woman is defending her health, her peace of mind, her way of life against an unwanted intruder. If a stranger tried to take these things away from her against her will, might she not be justified in exercising her right to self-defense? Legal tradition upholds that idea—the notion of abortion to save the life of the mother.

Of course, if the fetus has an absolute "right to life," as some would say, then even if the mother's life is at stake, the abortion should not be performed. Not ever. No exceptions. If that were true for me, I would never have done the first one.

But there are always exceptions. What about ectopic pregnancies? We destroy such pregnancies because they're not viable. An embryo that attaches itself outside the uterus can cause internal damage, bleeding, even the woman's death. Nowadays, with microsurgery, we can remove an embryo from a fallopian tube, saving the tube and possibly the woman's reproductive function. The alternative is waiting for rupture—a certainty in medicine. There are cases on record where hospitals, bound by religious convictions and not permitting abortion, also do not permit a gynecologist to remove an eccyesis [the embryo in an ectopic pregnancy] until it has been ruptured—and is therefore no longer "alive."

In an era in which fertilized ova in a petri dish can be called "children" in a court of law, will ectopic pregnancies, too, have a "right to life"?

Exposing the "Abortion Is Murder" Argument

One fascinating dilemma in the abortion debate is the right to abortion in cases of rape or incest. If an embryo is a person and abortion is murder and no one has the constitutional right to kill another person, how can it be OK to kill only at certain times— as in rape or incest? Isn't killing always wrong? If, indeed, it is a killing? Is it murder sometimes and not murder at others?

It seems that people who say they're against abortion except in cases of rape or incest are basing their judgment on something other than whether or not abortion is killing. Clearly, their feelings about abortion have to do not with the "innocent life" of the embryo or fetus, but with the mother. The idea of forcing a woman or girl to carry the product of rape to term is repugnant to most people. Not to all, just most. When pressed, they'll say that they're against abortion for "birth control," but not in cases of rape or incest, because then the woman didn't "intend" to get pregnant—she was an "innocent victim." Rationalization to fit an accepted scheme? You tell me.

Presumably, then, at other times the woman isn't "innocent." It's a case, if you'll pardon the expression, of "She made her bed, now let her lie in it"—she "chose" to get pregnant, or at least to put herself at risk for pregnancy by having sex, playing what in the pre-pill days used to be called "Vatican roulette." The logical conclusion to that thought is ". . . which she *shouldn't have done* if she didn't want to get pregnant." She's been irresponsible. Now let's see that she pays for it. A lot of the arguments about abortion are really about controlling women's sexuality or just controlling women, period.

And as far as "using abortion for birth control" goes, it's a red herring. American women don't, and in our almost quarter-century of legalized abortion there are no signs that it is a factor. In some of the Eastern Bloc countries after World War II, where birth control was hard to come by, women had a dozen or more abortions. That's using abortion for birth control, and it hasn't happened here. We see women who are mostly responsible, who have maybe a thirty-minute lapse. Are we supposed to say to them, "The punishment for that is the next eighteen years of your life"? We see teenagers getting pregnant because they're naive, or because they can't get birth control at all. Why not? Because they "should" be abstinent.

Pregnancy as an Invasion

[A] metaphor that counters the devaluation of women by anti-abortion forces can be found in *Alien*, that ultimate sci-fi horror story of the reproductive cycle. In the film, the offspring of an unwanted pregnancy is portrayed as an intruder into the last frontier of inner space, resembling a penis with teeth bursting out of the chest cavity in a kind of equal-opportunity Caesarean. Has there ever been a more graphic statement of the unspoken facts of fertility? "Many women, good mothers, who become unwillingly pregnant, speak of the fetus they carry as an invader, a tumor, a thing to be removed," Sallie Tisdale wrote in a sobering meditation in *Vogue* on the reproductive experience as an act of invasion as much as love. Whatever moral status may be ascribed to an unborn child—alien invader, innocent human being, or a person with a right to life—no one has the right to use another's body as a life support system without her consent. It is time to recognize the murder case against abortion for what it is: a stupendous vaudeville of moral folly.

Paul Savoy, *Tikkun*, September/October 1993.

Former Surgeon General C. Everett Koop summed it up: "We are at a very strange place in history where the people most opposed to abortions are also most opposed to the one thing that would stop them, which is contraceptive information.". . .

Choice and Rights

"You're really talking about having a choice, aren't you?" Jessica asked. "It's my frog, and I don't want to kill it. I don't want to be forced to do something I don't want to do. And I'm glad they can't make me—because they can't, can they? If I'm willing to take the consequences, I can do what I want."

"As far as your frog goes, yes. As long as you understand what you're doing."

"I know. It's my class, my grade and my frog. It's up to me to decide what to do. I really don't want to kill the frog. But . . ."

I turned to Jessica and wanted to pick her brain, now that she had gotten mine churning away.

"Jess, what about your classmates? Do you think ill of them because they want to experiment and haven't even considered the consequences to their frogs?"

"Well, gosh, it would be better if there were more of us protesting, wouldn't it? We could make more noise. I did try to convince my friend Martha to refuse to kill her frog. Yeah, maybe I was kinda strong about it." She grimaced. "I called her a 'frog killer' and stuff. And said she had no respect for life. Come to think of it, she's still a little mad."

I was going in the direction I wanted.

"Jess, dear, was that right of you? Weren't you trying to force your morals and ethics, your thinking, onto Martha? Did she deserve any name-calling at all? You just used words. But suppose you felt even stronger. Would you have taken Martha's frog away from her—even forced her bodily away from her frog? What about your other classmates? Should they be allowed to kill their frogs?"

"I did think of setting all the frogs free. Maybe taking them down to the pond. Just to show people I meant it."

"Why didn't you?"

"Well, there's this guy in my class who's a real science nerd, you know—"

"Like your uncle."

"Worse. And he's got a chance at a big science prize, and scholarships and stuff, and I could have messed that up. He's a nerd, but even so—"

"But if you really meant it, as you say, why not grab all the frogs and lock the door to the biology lab? Would you be justified in defending the frog tank with a baseball bat, or spilling catsup on your teacher's car to simulate frog's blood? Would you chain yourself to the frog tank so nobody could get to a frog?"

"Hey, wait a minute. I'm talking about me—my frog. No one else's. They have rights too, don't they?"

I was never prouder of my niece.

I thought of that Thanksgiving Day session with Jessica years later when I saw a clever bumper sticker on a station wagon driven by a mother with her five children, a bumper sticker that said it all for me—"Against Abortion? Don't have one."

*"By abortion, the mother does not learn to love,
but kills even her own child to solve her problems."*

Abortion Is a
Selfish Choice

Mother Teresa

Mother Teresa is the founder and mother superior of the Order
of the Missionaries of Charity, which provides services to needy
people around the world. The following viewpoint is excerpted
from a speech she gave at a National Prayer Breakfast in Washington, D.C., on February 3, 1994. Mother Teresa argues that
those who choose abortion are making a selfish choice. Abortion destroys one's ability to love, she contends, because people
who choose abortion do so to avoid the hurt that unselfish love
of their children would require.

As you read, consider the following questions:

1. According to Mother Teresa, why is abortion a great destroyer
   of peace?
2. Why does abortion lead to violence, in the author's view?
3. In Mother Teresa's opinion, how can the problem of
   unwanted children be solved?

Excerpted from "Mother Teresa Goes to Washington," *Crisis*, March 1994, a reprint of
Mother Teresa's speech at the National Prayer Breakfast, February 3, 1994; courtesy of the
Missionaries of Charity.

I can never forget the experience I had in visiting a home where they kept all these old parents of sons and daughters who had just put them into an institution and forgotten them—maybe. I saw that in that home these old people had everything—good food, comfortable place, television, everything, but everyone was looking toward the door. And I did not see a single one with a smile on his face. I turned to Sister and I asked: "Why do these people who have every comfort here, why are they all looking toward the door? Why are they not smiling?"

I am so used to seeing the smiles on our people, even the dying ones smile. And Sister said: "This is the way it is nearly every day. They are expecting, they are hoping that a son or daughter will come to visit them. They are hurt because they are forgotten." And see, this neglect to love brings spiritual poverty. Maybe in our own family we have somebody who is feeling lonely, who is feeling sick, who is feeling worried. Are we there? Are we willing to give until it hurts in order to be with our families, or do we put our own interests first? These are the questions we must ask ourselves, especially as we begin this year of the family [1994]. We must remember that love begins at home and we must also remember that "the future of humanity passes through the family."

Breaking the Peace

I was surprised in the West to see so many young boys and girls given to drugs. And I tried to find out why. Why is it like that, when those in the West have so many more things than those in the East? And the answer was: "Because there is no one in the family to receive them." Our children depend on us for everything—their health, their nutrition, their security, their coming to know and love God. For all of this, they look to us with trust, hope and expectation. But often father and mother are so busy they have no time for their children, or perhaps they are not even married or have given up on their marriage. So the children go to the streets and get involved in drugs or other things. We are talking of love of the child, which is where love and peace must begin. These are the things that break peace.

But I feel that the greatest destroyer of peace today is abortion, because it is a war against the child, a direct killing of the innocent child, murder by the mother herself. And if we accept that a mother can kill even her own child, how can we tell other people not to kill one another? How do we persuade a woman not to have an abortion? As always, we must persuade her with love and we remind ourselves that love means to be willing to give until it hurts. Jesus gave even His life to love us. So, the mother who is thinking of abortion, should be helped to love, that is, to give until it hurts her plans, or her free time, to respect the life of her child. The father of that child, whoever he is, must also give until it hurts.

Abortion Leads to Violence

By abortion, the mother does not learn to love, but kills even her own child to solve her problems. And, by abortion, the father is told that he does not have to take any responsibility at all for the child he has brought into the world. That father is likely to put other women into the same trouble. So abortion just leads to more abortion. Any country that accepts abortion is not teaching its people to love, but to use any violence to get what they want. This is why the greatest destroyer of love and peace is abortion.

© Cullum/Copley News Service. Reprinted with permission.

Many people are very, very concerned with the children of India, with the children of Africa where quite a few die of hunger, and so on. Many people are also concerned about all the violence in this great country of the United States. These concerns are very good. But often these same people are not concerned with the millions who are being killed by the deliberate decision of their own mothers. And this is what is the greatest destroyer of peace today—abortion which brings people to such blindness.

And for this I appeal in India and I appeal everywhere—"Let us bring the child back." The child is God's gift to the family. Each child is created in the special image and likeness of God for greater things—to love and to be loved. In this year of the family we must bring the child back to the center of our care and concern. This is the only way that our world can survive because our children are the only hope for the future. As older people are called to God, only their children can take their places.

But what does God say to us? He says: "Even if a mother could forget her child, I will not forget you. I have carved you in the palm of my hand." We are carved in the palm of His hand; that unborn child has been carved in the hand of God from conception and is called by God to love and to be loved, not only now in this life, but forever. God can never forget us.

Adoption, Not Abortion

I will tell you something beautiful. We are fighting abortion by adoption—by care of the mother and adoption for her baby. We have saved thousands of lives. We have sent word to the clinics, to the hospitals and police stations: "Please don't destroy the child; we will take the child." So we always have someone tell the mothers in trouble: "Come, we will take care of you, we will get a home for your child." And we have a tremendous demand from couples who cannot have a child—but I never give a child to a couple who have done something not to have a child. Jesus said, "Anyone who receives a child in my name, receives me." By adopting a child, these couples receive Jesus but, by aborting a child, a couple refuses to receive Jesus.

Please don't kill the child. I want the child. Please give me the child. I am willing to accept any child who would be aborted and to give that child to a married couple who will love the child and be loved by the child. From our children's home in Calcutta alone, we have saved over 3000 children from abortion. These children have brought such love and joy to their adopting parents and have grown up so full of love and joy.

I know that couples have to plan their family and for that there is natural family planning. The way to plan the family is natural family planning, not contraception. In destroying the power of giving life, through contraception, a husband or wife is doing something to self. This turns the attention to self and so it destroys the gift of love in him or her. In loving, the husband and wife must turn their attention to each other as happens in natural family planning, and not to self, as happens in contraception. Once that living love is destroyed by contraception, abortion follows very easily.

I also know that there are great problems in the world—that many spouses do not love each other enough to practice natural

51

family planning. We cannot solve all the problems in the world, but let us never bring in the worst problem of all, and that is to destroy love. And this is what happens when we tell people to practice contraception and abortion.

The poor are very great people. They can teach us so many beautiful things. Once one of them came to thank us for teaching her natural family planning and said: "You people who have practiced chastity, you are the best people to teach us natural family planning because it is nothing more than self-control out of love for each other." And what this poor person said is very true. These poor people maybe have nothing to eat, maybe they have not a home to live in, but they can still be great people when they are spiritually rich.

When I pick up a person from the street, hungry, I give him a plate of rice, a piece of bread. But a person who is shut out, who feels unwanted, unloved, terrified, the person who has been thrown out of society—that spiritual poverty is much harder to overcome. And abortion, which often follows from contraception, brings a people to be spiritually poor, and that is the worst poverty and the most difficult to overcome.

"No woman should feel guilty about terminating an unwanted pregnancy."

Abortion Is Not a Selfish Choice

Revolutionary Worker

In the following viewpoint, the *Revolutionary Worker*, a publication of the Revolutionary Communist Party, argues that the fundamental issue in the abortion debate is the right of women to make their own decisions about reproduction. A woman who decides to have an abortion because it is not a good time to have a child is not making a selfish decision, the *Revolutionary Worker* maintains, because a woman's physical and mental health and her right to function fully in society take priority over reproduction.

As you read, consider the following questions:

1. What is one of the ways in which oppressive societies have controlled women, according to the *Revolutionary Worker*?
2. In the view of the *Revolutionary Worker*, why is the state's claim that it has a vested interest in protecting the life of an unborn child false?
3. What is the result when women are allowed to control their own reproduction, according to the author?

Revolutionary Worker, "A Revolutionary Communist Viewpoint on Abortion and Women's Liberation," January 15, 1995. Reprinted by permission of RCP Publications, Chicago. Subheadings and boxed quotation added to original by Greenhaven Press.

Debating whether women should have the right to abortion is like debating whether Black people should have the right not to be slaves. It's that fundamental a question.

A Life and Death Issue

It is a life and death issue. People on both sides of the barricades in this battle feel very strongly about this question exactly because it raises larger questions about the social relations between men and women and the whole way society is organized. But there is a right and wrong side to the argument.

The anti-abortionists argue abortion is murder because "fetuses are unborn children." And they say "the life of the fetus" is central to the abortion debate. But this is a lie.

> I resent anti-abortionists calling themselves "pro-life." To me human life goes beyond a few living cells. What would "life" be without intelligence and goals and dreams? It is NOT the goal and dream of every woman to have babies, and having babies may irrevocably interfere with some women's visions of their lives.
>
> A woman in Boston

History has shown that one of the main ways oppressive societies have established control over women is to control women's reproduction. From the time human societies became divided along property lines and male dominance was imposed over the family and society, the right to make decisions about reproduction has been taken away from women. The church and the state dictate women's subservience to men. And religious and political institutions, laws, and the weight of reactionary ideology all work together as a coercive weight on women. And yet women have never ceased to resist this coercion.

The state claims it has a "vested interest" in protecting the life of "pre-born" Americans. But what is this vested interest? Surely not some selfless interest in children in general! Millions of children in the United States suffer from lack of adequate health care, nutrition, day care, education, etc., as a matter of routine and as a direct result of this system's policies. Millions of children around the world suffer the terrible repercussions of U.S. imperialist policies ranging from starvation to the ravages of war. So what is this "vested interest"? It can only be a vested interest in regulating the lives and actions of women.

This is a stark example of how property relations—which lie at the heart of capitalist society—are also at the heart of the abortion issue. From the point of view of those who run this country, women are property to be controlled. And fetuses are property that has become politically and ideologically very useful in their efforts to put women down.

There are many different reasons why women get abortions.

And they are all valid. No woman should feel guilty about terminating an unwanted pregnancy. And no woman should buy the crap that having an abortion is "selfish."

The birth of a child can be a source of great joy to a woman. But it can be a nightmare for a woman who *for whatever reason* does not want to have a child at a particular time or under particular circumstances. In such cases *forcing* a woman to continue a pregnancy is extremely cruel and sadistic. It will affect her entire life, and no woman's life should be twisted in such a way. No child should be born unwanted. No woman should be forced to choose between compulsory motherhood and a back-alley butcher.

Banning abortion is like rape—the violent assertion of male domination and male supremacist society over women, the forceful and violent control of women's bodies, in the most personal dimensions. Banning abortion means suppression of women by force of law and the state. It is institutionalized violence against women.

A Sacrificial Act

Abortion is a mother's act. It is an act of sacrifice, love, power, and necessity. . . .

It does stop a beating heart, but it also keeps another one going: the heart and the life of each woman who chooses it. It does that too.

Merle Hoffman, *On the Issues*, Winter 1996.

Today the right to abortion is still legal in the United States. But restrictive state laws and the attacks of anti-abortion forces are making it harder and harder for women to exercise this right. There are fewer doctors performing abortions. The result of this will mean that instead of going in early for a simple and safe medical procedure, many women will find themselves trapped—forced to wait for later and more difficult abortions, forced to bear unwanted children, or forced to swallow poisons, mutilate themselves with coat hangers, or die at the hands of fast-buck butchers. All this was routine in the United States prior to 1973 and continues to be routine in many parts of the world today.

Abortion is a common and significant part of women's having control over their own lives. And women have to stop being defensive about it. No matter how late in a pregnancy, no matter how much it *might* be able to live outside a woman's body, a fetus is NOT a child. And abortion is NOT murder.

"Life" is a characteristic of everything on this planet which is capable of growth, development, active transformation of its environment, reproduction, etc. It is characteristic of every animal, every plant, and every cell for that matter. A fertilized egg is "alive." But so is a human ovum, a human sperm cell, or a human skin cell! Obviously every living thing cannot and should not be preserved.

A Fetus Is Not a Child

A pregnancy is a nine-month process during which a fertilized egg grows, develops and goes through a series of transformations before it can finally become a baby—a new human being—*at the time of its birth.* BEFORE birth, it is not a child or a person with an independent existence. It is a developing mass of tissue integrally connected to the woman's vital biological processes. It is part of that woman with no separate social existence. It has the *potential* to become human. But it is not yet a separate social being that should have separate social rights. For that it must have entered society as a separate entity. That is, it must have been born.

Here lies the heart of the struggle around abortion: As long as reproduction is rooted in individual women, the basis exists for the social regulation of reproduction to be an oppressive thing for women. Exactly because of this, the overall physical and social well-being of women must take priority over any subordinate processes, such as reproduction. This is a question of women's health. But even more, it is a question of *women's right to function fully in society.*

A woman who is forced to bear a child against her will is assaulted and degraded in body and spirit. On the other hand, a woman who can control her own reproduction and decide whether and when to have children will be stronger, more independent, and better able to deal with the world at large, outside the confines of the family. She will be better able to lift her head, better able to dream and visualize the way the world COULD BE. And she will be better able to act to realize these dreams. Stronger women make stronger fighters, for themselves, for their children, for all the women, men, and children everywhere who have known conditions of oppression.

Periodical Bibliography

The following articles have been selected to supplement the diverse views presented in this chapter. Addresses are provided for periodicals not indexed in the *Readers' Guide to Periodical Literature*, the *Alternative Press Index*, or the *Social Sciences Index*.

Hadley Arkes — "Abortion Facts and Feelings," *First Things*, April 1994. Available from PO Box 3000, Dept. FT, Denville, NJ 07834.

J. Bottum — "Facing Up to Infanticide," *First Things*, February 1996.

Mona Charen — "A New Moral View on Abortion?" *Conservative Chronicle*, January 19, 1994. Available from Box 29, Hampton, IA 50441.

Candace C. Crandall — "The Fetus Beat Us," *Women's Quarterly*, Winter 1996. Available from 2111 Wilson Blvd., Suite 550, Arlington, VA 22201-3057.

Crisis — "Another January 22," January 1994. Available from PO Box 1006, Notre Dame, IN 46556.

Ronald M. Dworkin — "Life Is Sacred. That's the Easy Part," *New York Times Magazine*, May 16, 1993.

Ellen Wilson Fielding — "Going Far Enough," *Human Life Review*, Spring 1994. Available from 150 E. 35th St., Rm. 840, New York, NY 10016.

Paul Greenberg — "Culture of Death," *Weekly Standard*, October 9, 1995. Available from PO Box 96153, Washington, DC 20090-6153.

James W. Huston — "Just When Is Killing a Fetus Murder?" *Human Life Review*, Fall 1994.

Ralph McInerny — "Choice," *Crisis*, February 1995.

William Murchison — "Middle Class Amorality," *Human Life Review*, Fall 1995.

Charley Reese — "The Boundaries of Abortion," *Conservative Chronicle*, December 21, 1994.

James Q. Wilson — "On Abortion," *Commentary*, January 1994.

Naomi Wolf — "Our Bodies, Our Souls," *New Republic*, October 16, 1995.

Should Abortion Rights Be Restricted?

Abortion

Chapter Preface

Like many teenage girls facing unpleasant news, "Mary Smith," a 15-year-old from Blair, Nebraska, tried to deny the fact that she was pregnant. By the time she finally confirmed her pregnancy with a home test in September 1994, she was more than five months pregnant. When she told her parents of her pregnancy, the Smiths immediately scheduled an appointment for her at an abortion clinic.

Mary's 16-year-old boyfriend, Heath Mayfield, did not approve of the abortion and tried to talk her out of having the procedure. Heath's parents, John and Cathy Tull, also wanted to change Mary's mind about the abortion, but Mary's parents refused to let them talk with her. So the Tulls did the only thing they could think of to stop Mary from having an abortion—they had her arrested.

Cathy Tull convinced a local doctor who had never seen Mary to sign a letter stating that an elective abortion "could not only be harmful . . . but even in the most extreme case be potentially fatal to the mother." Armed with this letter, Tull went to the police, who, citing "the health risk to Mary if an abortion was performed," took Mary into custody to prevent her from having an abortion. At a juvenile court hearing two days later, Mary's parents agreed that Mary, who was determined to be 27 weeks pregnant, was too far along in her pregnancy for an abortion to be safe. Mary gave birth to a girl on December 7, 1994.

Although the U.S. Supreme Court has allowed states to require minors who want an abortion to obtain parental consent or to notify their parents about their decision, it has struck down similar laws that required the consent or notification of the woman's husband or the baby's father. Therefore, Heath Mayfield and the Tulls had no legal authority to prevent Mary's abortion. The Tulls maintain that they were merely trying to exercise their right to free speech and Heath's right to express his concerns and convictions to Mary. The Smiths contend that they had the right to make their decision privately without interference from Heath, the Tulls, or city officials.

Much of the debate over abortion centers around who should have a say in the decision to abort: the pregnant woman, the parents of teenage girls, the father, or the state. Some abortion rights proponents argue that a woman's right to abortion should not be restricted in any way, but many Americans favor such restrictions as banning late-term abortions and requiring a 24-hour waiting period before an abortion can be performed. The viewpoints in the following chapter present differing views on whether abortion rights should be restricted.

"Congress could certainly justify legislation prohibiting abortions after the beginning of the second trimester."

Abortion Should Be Restricted

Stephen C. Meyer and David K. DeWolf

The age of fetal viability continues to drop, maintain Stephen C. Meyer and David K. DeWolf in the following viewpoint, and science has shown that fetuses as young as eight weeks can feel pain. These facts would give Congress justification for prohibiting abortions after the onset of fetal viability or during the second or third trimester, they contend. Restricting these types of abortion is the logical first step toward banning all abortions, the authors argue. Meyer is an associate professor of religion and philosophy at Whitworth College in Spokane, Washington. DeWolf is an associate professor of law at Gonzaga Law School in Spokane.

As you read, consider the following questions:

1. In 1994 how many abortions were performed after the onset of fetal viability, according to Meyer and DeWolf?
2. What is the only reason that abortion has been permitted by the Supreme Court, in the authors' opinion?
3. In the authors' view, why should pro-life activists model their campaign to ban abortions on Abraham Lincoln's strategy concerning slavery?

Excerpted from Stephen C. Meyer and David K. DeWolf, "Fetal Position," *National Review*, March 20, 1995; ©1995 by National Review, Inc., 150 E. 35th St., New York, NY 10016. Reprinted by permission.

The moral case for limiting late-term abortions depends not solely on religious authority but also on widely shared moral intuitions and recent developments in medical science. With the advance of medical technology since the 1970s, the age at which a human fetus can survive outside its mother's womb—the so-called age of viability—has steadily declined. While obstetricians disagree about the minimum age of viability, all agree that some premature infants of 20 weeks, and most of 24 weeks, can survive *ex utero*. Yet under *Roe* v. *Wade*, clinical abortion is allowed through the full nine months of pregnancy. In 1994, more than 50,000 abortions were performed in the United States after 17 weeks' gestation, including at least 17,000 after the point of viability.

Legalized Infanticide

While such abortions constitute a small minority of the 1.6 million performed annually, they represent little more than legalized infanticide. As many as 1.5 million American families are waiting to adopt children. Women wanting to rid themselves of viable infants can generally do so as easily by delivering them and then turning them over to adoptive parents as by aborting them. Given the health risks to women from the abortion procedure itself, it is hard to provide a compelling reason (apart from complications that threaten the mother's life) to allow abortion late in pregnancy.

In any case, the present situation creates absurd moral dilemmas for those defending the status quo. What possible justification can exist for the termination of an unwanted fetus of, say seven months, when heroic medical measures are being taken, possibly in the next ward, to save even younger children at their parents' behest? Why should the biological mother's attitude determine an infant's moral status? Those who deny the Biblical claim that God "forms the spirit of man within him" may still dispute the sanctity of life or whether life begins at conception. But no one can credibly claim that life begins only after a full nine months of gestation.

Advances in medical science and technology have important moral implications for mid-term abortions as well. So disturbing has been the experience of observing abortion on ultrasound monitors that many abortion doctors who have seen the procedure have refused to participate in abortions again. Bernard Nathanson, a former director of the National Abortion Rights Action League (NARAL), who performed thousands of abortions, repudiated the practice in the early 1980s after observing the apparent agony of a fetus subjected to a suction-tip abortion.

Modern neurology supports Nathanson's impression that the fetus experiences pain, not just reflex. Reflexive reactions, such as the involuntary and painless knee kick elicited by the tap of a physician's mallet, electrically stimulate only the spinal column. By contrast, the more complex "aversive" reactions that indicate pain stimulate a tiny brain sensor called the thalamus. Neurologists can detect thalamus and central-nervous-system function in the human fetus as early as the 8th, and certainly by the 13th, week of gestation. The coordinated motor responses observable in a fetus undergoing abortion—its desperate rearing and "silent screams"—give every indication that the second-trimester fetus is a sentient creature capable of experiencing pain.

Americans Support Abortion Restrictions

According to a Gallup survey, 73 percent of Americans support a prohibition on abortion after the first trimester of pregnancy (about ten weeks after conception). This survey shows that 82 percent of those who are strongly pro-life, as well as 82 percent of those in the middle, would support such a proposal. More surprisingly, even 46 percent of those identified as strongly pro-choice agree that abortion should be limited to the first trimester.

Other polls have consistently shown that, while a majority of Americans support a woman's right to choose an abortion in the early weeks of pregnancy, a majority also believe that at some point the government acquires the right to intervene to protect the life of the unborn child.

Steven R. Hemler, Richard G. Wilkins, and Frank H. Fischer, *National Review*, December 27, 1993.

By what moral calculus, religious or secular, can such a procedure be justified? Humanitarian common sense dictates that we not subject sentient human fetuses to painful procedures that we would protest if they were done to the higher animals. We would not heedlessly dismember dogs or cats or crush their skulls with forceps. Why shouldn't a sentient and, by all accounts, at least a potential human being be afforded the same considerations and legal protection as animals receive in many states?

In view of these considerations, a future Congress could certainly justify legislation prohibiting abortions after the beginning of the second trimester (13 weeks). For the present, however, pro-life legislators should focus on prohibiting post-viability abortions and educating the public about the physiological development of the pre-viability fetus and its affective response to the abortion procedure. Congress could, for example, fund programs designed to inform prospective parents about fetal pain and post-abortion health risks to the mother. Those worried that such a move would create a political opportunity for pro-choice Democrats should note that more than 80 per cent of the public, including a significant percentage of the population usually classified in polls as "pro-choice," already opposes abortions after the beginning of the second trimester.

The Significance of *Casey*

On the legal front, there are reasons for cautious optimism about national legislative efforts that occupy the moral and political center of the abortion controversy. The "center" or "plurality" of the Supreme Court (David Souter, Anthony Kennedy, and Sandra Day O'Connor), which has to approve the constitutionality of any legislative restrictions on abortion, upheld some limits in *Planned Parenthood of Southeastern Pennsylvania* v. *Casey*. Although they claimed to reaffirm the central holding of *Roe*, they effectively redefined its meaning and undermined its logical and moral foundation.

In *Roe*, the Court said the mother's rights are strongest in the first trimester, but it did not accept that the rights of the fetus ever eclipsed those of the mother. In *Casey*, the Court explicitly rejected this reasoning, with seven of the nine Justices allowing some limitations on abortion rights. As the plurality put it, "States are free to enact laws that provide a reasonable framework for women to make a decision that has such a profound and lasting meaning," provided they do not place an "undue burden" on the woman. More importantly, the plurality also acknowledged that, while "the woman has some freedom to terminate her pregnancy," that freedom gives way at some point to the rights of the fetus. In particular, they said "the line should be drawn at viability."

It remains true, of course, that the center, and thus the Court, refused to overturn *Roe*. Yet the center's reasons for refusing to do so suggest a greater openness to shifting policy responsibility from the Court back to legislatures. The Court seemed reluctant to overturn *Roe* because it worried about the absence of ballast in the political center. The plurality called for "the contending sides of a national controversy to end their national division by accepting a common mandate rooted in the Constitution."

Pro-life legislators can take the plurality's concern about moderation into account and formulate their legislative agenda accordingly. They certainly should feel no compunction about occupying the territory that has already been ceded by the Court. Abortions after 20 weeks (the point of earliest viability) remain legal in all fifty states, even though a majority (at least six) of the Court's current members have indicated a willingness to consider legislation protecting viable life.

Yet constitutional opportunities may exist for legislation that presses the issue further. The Court's abandonment of the original justification for *Roe* may allow the emergence of a new legal context for the discussion of abortion—one that could allow restrictions on sex selection and the abortion of sentient second-trimester infants.

Banning Abortions

If . . . there developed a consensus as to when an embryo became a baby, should the law recognize this and ban abortions after that period? I believe that it should, provided there were exceptions for grave and special cases (such as a severe deformity), and even then only after the woman had obtained the advice and consent of disinterested and expert parties.

James Q. Wilson, *Commentary*, January 1994.

In *Roe*, the Supreme Court acknowledged that, if the fetus was indeed a person, it would be protected by the Fourteenth Amendment. Abortion has been permitted only because of doubts about the personhood of the fetus. Yet with the advance of medical technology and the science of fetology, arguments denying the personhood of the 20-week, and indeed the 13-week, fetus seem increasingly implausible. Hence, the Fourteenth Amendment—which authorizes Congress to intervene on behalf of "persons" in danger of being deprived of life, liberty, or equal protection—emerges as a legitimate vehicle for protecting the unborn.

In previous civil-rights legislation Congress has outlawed race and sex discrimination. What greater form of sex discrimination could exist than selective killing on the basis of sex?

Tackling the sex-selection and fetal-pain issues will push the envelope of opportunity detectable in *Casey*. While there is a danger of overreaching, there is also a danger of timidity. If Congress cannot persuade the Supreme Court to retreat gracefully from its attempts to micromanage the abortion controversy, what are the chances that the Court will do so as a result of piecemeal state legislation? In fact, Congress has the opportunity to shoulder more responsibility for abortion policy and to wean the Court from a task for which it increasingly displays only a sense of weary obligation. Congress can offer itself as a lightning rod for the political repercussions that centrists on the Court fear. . . .

Limitations, Then Abolition

Many pro-life activists may feel uneasy about appearing to compromise on the sanctity of life at any point after conception.

In this connection, an historical parallel may prove instructive. While debating Stephen Douglas, and later while campaigning for the Presidency, Abraham Lincoln acknowledged that the Federal Government did not have the power to end slavery by fiat. Yet by warning that "a house divided against itself cannot stand," he refused to admit the legitimacy of slavery. He continued to argue, on Biblical and moral grounds, for ultimate abolition. At the same time, in the legal and political domain he accepted compromises designed to achieve limited goals and to build moral consensus.

By refusing to press for immediate and outright abolition in the South, Lincoln angered many abolitionists; by supporting limits on the territorial expansion of slavery, he angered slave owners, who understood that such measures denied the moral legitimacy of slavery. Ever principled *and* pragmatic, Lincoln forced the issue where the arguments for slavery were weakest and avoided engagement (until he could win) where justifications for slavery appeared most strong.

Pro-life legislators have an opportunity to employ this venerable Republican strategy to redefine the terms of the most compelling moral issue of our time. By passing intentionally modest and incremental legislation designed to expose the moral contradictions, the legal ambiguities, and the political vulnerabilities inherent in the pro-choice position, Republicans can begin to forge a national consensus against the unnecessary killing of the unborn. Not only would legislation of this sort expose the anachronistic legal and scientific reasoning that remains the sole foundation for *Roe*, it could also force both political parties to acknowledge the moral consensus that *Roe* has forcibly suppressed. Americans believe that abortion ought to be made more rare. Republicans who heard and understood this message from the election of 1994 will survive to run again and again—as will American children yet unborn.

"The movement to newly restrict reproductive choice is . . . a grave threat to all Americans' cherished right to privacy, bodily integrity and religious liberty."

Abortion Should Not Be Restricted

American Civil Liberties Union

The American Civil Liberties Union (ACLU) is a national organization that works to defend civil rights guaranteed by the U.S. Constitution. In the following viewpoint, the ACLU argues that several constitutional amendments guarantee American women the right to have an abortion. This constitutional right should not be restricted because bans on abortion threaten women's health, discriminate against women, and violate the First Amendment's guarantee of religious liberty.

As you read, consider the following questions:

1. The right to abortion is guaranteed under what amendments, in the ACLU's opinion?
2. Why did abortion become illegal in the nineteenth century, according to the ACLU?
3. According to the ACLU, how are "fetal rights" used to deny women their rights?

Adapted from "Reproductive Freedom—the Right to Choose: A Fundamental Liberty," ACLU *Briefing Paper* no. 15; ©1992, the American Civil Liberties Union. Reprinted with permission.

The Bill of Rights of the United States Constitution guarantees individuals the right to personal autonomy, which means that a person's decisions regarding his or her personal life are none of the government's business. That right, which is part of the right to privacy, encompasses decisions about parenthood, including a woman's right to decide for herself whether to complete or terminate a pregnancy, as well as the right to use contraception, freedom from forced sterilization and freedom from employment discrimination based on childbearing capacity.

As early as 1923, the U.S. Supreme Court ruled that the Constitution protects personal decisions regarding marriage and the family from governmental intrusion. In 1965, the Court ruled that a state cannot prohibit a married couple from practicing contraception. In 1972, it extended the right to use birth control to all people, married or single. And in its 1973 ruling in *Roe v. Wade*, the Court held that the Constitution's protections of privacy as a fundamental right encompass a woman's decision to have an abortion.

The *Roe* decision, which legalized abortion nationwide, led to a dramatic improvement in the lives and health of women. Before *Roe*, women experiencing unwanted or crisis pregnancies faced the perils and indignities of self-induced abortion, back-alley abortion, or forced childbirth. Today, *Roe* protects the right of women to make life choices in keeping with their conscience or religious beliefs, consistent with American tradition. And by relieving American women of the burden of unwanted pregnancies, *Roe* has permitted them to pursue economic opportunities on a more equal basis with men.

The movement to newly restrict reproductive choice is, therefore, not only an attack on personal autonomy but also on the principle of equality for women, and it is a grave threat to all Americans' cherished right to privacy, bodily integrity and religious liberty.

Here are the American Civil Liberties Union's answers to questions frequently asked by the public about reproductive freedom and the Constitution.

How does the Constitution protect our right to privacy, including reproductive freedoms, if that right isn't explicitly named in the Constitution?

Even though a right to privacy is not named, the Ninth Amendment states that the naming of certain rights in the Constitution does not mean that other, unnamed rights are not "retained by the people." The Supreme Court has long held that the Bill of Rights protects certain liberties that, though unspecified, are "fundamental" to an individual's ability to function in society. These include the right to privacy, the right to travel, the right to vote and the right to marry. The Court has articulated various constitutional bases for these liberties, including the First, Fourth, Fifth, Ninth and Fourteenth Amendments. And in recent years, the Court has viewed the privacy right as an essential part of liberty, specifically protected by the Fifth and Fourteenth Amendments.

The Court has also held that the government may not restrict fundamental rights without a compelling reason, and it has repeatedly struck down various state restrictions on birth control and abortion as being unjustified by a compelling reason.

Abortion for Any Reason

Abortion is much easier, safer, cheaper and more available in the first months of pregnancy. And while everything should be done to facilitate a woman's choice in the first trimester, it is important to uphold the right of women to terminate an unwanted pregnancy at any time *for any reason*—and to provide women with the safest and least physically and emotionally demanding procedures available.

Mary Lou Greenberg, *Revolutionary Worker*, November 12, 1995.

Is reproductive choice protected by constitutional principles other than the right to privacy?

Although the Supreme Court has not so held, the ACLU believes that reproductive choice is not only protected by the right to privacy, but by several other constitutional principles, including the Fourteenth Amendment's guarantee of "equal protection of the laws" and the First Amendment's guarantee of freedom of religion.

Since only women can become pregnant, only women are affected by laws that dictate whether and under what conditions childbearing should occur. By limiting only women's right to make personal decisions, laws that prohibit or restrict abortion discriminate on the basis of sex in violation of the Fourteenth Amendment's Equal Protection Clause.

All of the world's major religions regard abortion as a theological issue, although their doctrines on the issue differ. Some religions teach that abortion is a sin; others, that it is a woman's duty if a pregnancy imperils her life or health. Bans on abortion force all citizens to conform to particular religious beliefs. Thus, the ACLU believes that such laws violate the First Amendment's Free Exercise Clause, which prohibits governmental encroachment on an individual's right to act according to her own beliefs or conscience. Abortion bans that establish, as a matter of law, that a fetus is a person violate the First Amendment's stricture against "an establishment of religion."

Have restrictions on abortion always existed?

No. Abortion was legal under common law—except in late pregnancy—for hundreds of years, including the period when our Constitution was written.

Not until the late 1800s did a movement seeking to curtail women's reproductive choices arise in the United States, spearheaded by two groups: Protestant nativists and medical doctors. The nativists opposed abortion out of fear that permitting limits on childbearing would cause the nation's white Protestant population to be "overrun" by immigrant Catholics, who had been entering the U.S. in great numbers since the 1830s and '40s. Doctors opposed it partly because they wanted to exclude midwives and traditional practitioners from performing abortions or any other medical practice, and partly because abortion in those days raised legitimate health concerns.

Societal changes also spurred opposition to abortion. The average size of families was shrinking, and the movement for women's suffrage and equality that had emerged in the 1840s was growing. These developments fueled fears of an imminent breakdown in women's purely domestic roles.

All of these factors prompted the passage of anti-abortion laws. But only in the late 20th century have anti-choice forces based their support for such laws on the concept of "protecting the fetus as a person."

Shouldn't the abortion question be left to state legislatures, or voted on by the people in referenda?

No. The Bill of Rights guarantees that fundamental rights cannot be abrogated by the will of the majority. For example, even if the majority of a state's citizens wanted to ban the practice of Catholicism, the constitutional right to free exercise of religion would forbid the legislature from enacting such a ban. Similarly, the privacy right that encompasses reproductive freedom, including the choices of abortion and contraception, cannot be overruled by referenda or legislation.

Moreover, we learned during the years before *Roe v. Wade* how women suffered in states where abortion was illegal. Affluent women were able to obtain safe abortions by traveling to states where they were legal, while poor, rural and young women—a disproportionate number of them women of color—were left to dangerous, back-alley abortions or forced childbirth. Such discriminatory conditions are unacceptable.

Do abortion bans also outlaw birth control?

Sometimes. Criminal abortion laws that define a fertilized egg as a "person" outlaw birth control methods that sometimes act to prevent pregnancy after fertilization, such as the intrauterine device (IUD), Norplant and the most popular birth control pill.

In addition, because abortion bans are criminal statutes that provide for long jail terms, when implemented they have a chilling effect on contraceptive research and other reproductive technologies, such as *in vitro* fertilization.

Separating Sex and Procreation

Not only are we fighting to win back funding and abortion rights for teenage women, today we must also resist the effort to overturn *Roe v. Wade*. *Roe* had a profound impact on the daily lives of women. Without legal abortion, thousands of women died in back alleys, thousands more suffered serious medical complications, and all women's health was threatened. After *Roe*, for those women who had access to legal abortion, a dangerous and desperate experience was transformed into a safe and legitimate health care option.

Together with legalizing contraception, abortion legitimized the separation between biology and procreation. This is a necessary step in the struggle for sexual freedom—heterosexual women could choose to have sex and choose not to be pregnant.

Marlene Gerber Fried and Loretta Ross, *Open Fire: The Open Magazine Pamphlet Series Anthology*, vol. 1, 1993.

Why are poor women and women of color especially hurt by anti-choice laws?

In 1972, before *Roe v. Wade*, 64 percent of the women who died from illegal abortion were women of color. Middle class and white women could more readily travel to obtain a legal abortion, pay a private physician to perform it, or convince typically all-white hospital committees that the procedure was necessary to preserve their mental health (one of the claims under which some states allowed abortion before *Roe*). Poor and nonwhite women would once again suffer, die or bear unwanted children in disproportionate numbers if the Supreme Court were to overturn *Roe*.

In addition, it is low-income women and, therefore, disproportionate numbers of non-white women, who suffer the most when the government prohibits the use of public funds for abortion and abortion information, or otherwise blocks women's access to abortion. Indeed the restrictive laws that govern public funding of medical care in effect coerce poor women to "choose" childbirth over abortion.

Why shouldn't the government be able to force a woman to carry a pregnancy to term for the sake of a fetus?

Our courts have always held that the government cannot compel an individual to use his or her body as an instrument for preserving people who are already born, much less for preserving a fetus in the womb. For example, the government cannot force a relative of a child afflicted with cancer to donate bone marrow or an organ to the child, even if the child is sure to die without the donation.

Obviously, if the state cannot force someone to undergo a bone marrow or organ transplant for a person already born, it cannot force a woman to continue a pregnancy that might entail great health risks for the sake of a fetus. As the Court of Appeals for the District of Columbia stated in a 1989 decision, "surely a fetus cannot have rights superior to those of a person who has already been born."

Enforcement of the idea that a fetus has legal rights superseding those of the woman who carries it would make pregnant women second class citizens with fewer rights, and more obligations, than others. Moreover, application of the "fetal rights" concept has already had devastating effects on women's right to bodily integrity. For example, cancer patient Angela Carder, forced by the District of Columbia Superior Court to undergo a caesarean delivery of her 26-week-old fetus, died prematurely as a result. Under the banner of "fetal rights," pregnant women have been prosecuted for failing to follow medical advice, and even for failing to get to a hospital quickly enough after the onset of labor. The concept also inspired industrial employers to adopt "fetal protection" policies, whereby the capacity to become pregnant and pregnancy itself became the bases for closing off certain jobs to all women of childbearing age who refused to be sterilized. Fortunately, the Supreme Court struck down this discriminatory practice in a 1991 decision.

Shouldn't pregnant women who drink or use other drugs be prosecuted for "child abuse"?

Absolutely not, for several reasons. Prosecutions of women for their behavior during pregnancy threaten all women's rights because, again, they are based on the "fetal rights" concept. Acceptance of that concept in law could bring about government spying and restrictions on a wide range of private behavior, in the name of "fetal protection." Having one's privacy invaded would become the price of pregnancy.

Prosecutions of pregnant women for allegedly harming their fetuses through drug use contribute nothing to solving the problem of drug abuse. Instead, they create a climate of fear that deters pregnant women from seeking prenatal care, and from informing doctors about their drug use. The waste of taxpayers' money on these prosecutions is especially cynical, given the scarcity of prenatal care services for poor women.

Although 85 percent of the people who use drugs are white,

80 percent of the women criminally prosecuted for drug use during pregnancy are women of color. At least one study showed that African American women are ten times more likely than white women to be reported to civil authorities for allegedly harming a fetus by using drugs.

What would really help pregnant women, and help them deliver healthy babies, is access to affordable drug treatment programs. Pregnant women are often excluded from the few such programs that exist.

Why do laws requiring parental involvement in a minor's abortion decision infringe upon fundamental rights?

The Constitution protects all of us but especially those who are powerless to protect themselves. A minor who has good reasons for not wanting her parents to know she is pregnant is just such a powerless person.

Laws that require young women to inform their parents before obtaining an abortion are, at best, unnecessary since most young women automatically turn to their parents without prodding from the law. At worst, such laws are tragically misguided. Consider the plight of the underaged who become pregnant through incest (a 1970s study showed that, of girls 12 years old and younger seeking abortions, 65 percent were victims of incest). Confidentiality in such cases can be a life or death matter: In 1989, the day before she was scheduled to obtain an abortion, 13-year-old Spring Adams was shot to death by her father. Family members claimed he had been feeling guilty about impregnating his daughter.

Pregnant minors who cannot turn to their parents need extra legal protection that ensures their access to safe, confidential abortions, rather than laws that limit such access, since minors already face greater economic and privacy barriers to medical care than adult women do. . . .

In what ways have the opponents of choice attacked the right to choose abortion and birth control?

The right to choose has been under attack ever since contraception and abortion were first legalized. But the attacks have become more common and more extreme in recent years, in part because our last two Presidents [Ronald Reagan and George Bush] have supported them. They have taken the following forms:

• Opponents of choice have tried to limit the ability of federal or state health care programs to deliver abortion information and services to low-income women. First, in the late 1970s, Congress prohibited Medicaid coverage of abortion even though Medicaid fully funds all other health care, including childbirth. In 1980, the Supreme Court found this discriminatory policy to be constitutional. Since then, the federal government and many states have limited access to abortion and abortion information in a wide range of public programs. In 1991, the Supreme Court upheld federal regulations forbidding the staffs of family planning clinics that receive federal funds under Title X of the Public Health Service Act from providing their patients with accurate information about, or referrals for, abortion.

• States have erected such obstacles as mandatory waiting periods, restrictions on late abortions, parental notification/consent laws and laws that force doctors to give anti-abortion lectures, or that require married women to involve their husbands in their abortion choice. These laws directly restrict women's right to choose and, by increasing medical costs and physicians' liability, make access to abortion more difficult.

• Some states (Louisiana and Utah, for example) have enacted laws that criminalize nearly all abortions. These laws literally turn back the clock to the days before *Roe* when physicians, and sometimes patients, faced jail for performing and seeking abortions.

What can I do to help protect reproductive choice?

Congress can pass a constitutional amendment or enact a federal law, which would preempt state laws, to protect reproductive choice. You can help preserve the right to choose by urging your Congressional representatives to support federal protection of this right for all women, without exception . . . and by letting your state legislators know that you support reproductive choice. For more information, contact your local ACLU or the national ACLU Reproductive Freedom Project.

> *"I saw three of these partial-birth abortions up close. . . . It was the most horrifying experience of my life."*

Late-Term Abortion Should Be Banned

Brenda Shafer

Brenda Shafer is a registered nurse who participated in three late-term (or partial-birth) abortions, all of which were performed on fetuses who were twenty-five weeks or older. In the following viewpoint, taken from a letter she wrote to Ohio congressman Tony Hall, Shafer describes the three abortions. While many abortion advocates claim this procedure is used only when the fetus has severe defects, Shafer contends that two of the three abortions she witnessed were performed not because the fetuses were deformed but because they were unwanted. Partial-birth abortions do not remove nonviable tissue but kill babies, she maintains, and therefore should be banned.

As you read, consider the following questions:

1. What reasons does Shafer give for agreeing to work for an abortion clinic?
2. How is a dilation and extraction (D&X) abortion different from a dilation and evacuation (D&E) abortion, according to the author?
3. According to Shafer, what made her change her mind about abortion?

Brenda Shafer, "What the Nurse Saw," *National Right to Life News*, July 18, 1995. Reprinted with permission.

Dear Congressman Tony Hall:

I read in the paper that you have sponsored a bill in Congress to make a law against what you call partial-birth abortions. [The Partial-Birth Abortion Ban Act (HR1833) passed both houses in 1995, but was vetoed by Bill Clinton in April 1996.] I encourage you to do everything you can to pass this law as soon as possible. I saw three of these partial-birth abortions up close in 1993. It was the most horrifying experience of my life.

I am a registered nurse with 13 years of experience. In September, 1993, I was working for a nursing agency. My employer asked me if I would accept an assignment to the Women's Medical Center, which is an abortion clinic in Dayton, run by Dr. Martin Haskell. I accepted the assignment because I was at that time very pro-choice. I had even told my two teenage daughters, who at that time were ages 14 and 17, that if one of them ever got pregnant at a young age, I would make them get an abortion. They disagreed with me on this and one of them even wrote an essay for a high school class about our differing views on the issue.

I worked as an assistant nurse at Dr. Haskell's clinic for three days. On the first day, we assisted in some first-trimester abortions, which is all I'd expected to be involved in. (I remember that one of the patients was a 15-year-old girl who was having her third abortion.)

On the second day, I saw Dr. Haskell do a second-trimester procedure that is called a D&E (dilation and evacuation). He used an ultrasound first to distinguish the different parts. Then he used forceps to pull apart the baby inside the uterus, bringing it out piece by piece, throwing the pieces in a pan. Also on the first two days, we inserted laminaria to dilate the cervixes of women who would receive late-term abortions a day or two later.

A Haunting Case

It was one of these cases that especially haunts me. The woman was six months pregnant (26½ weeks). A doctor told her that the baby had Down's syndrome and she decided to have an abortion. She came in the first two days to have the laminaria inserted and changed, and she cried the whole time. On the third day she came in to receive the partial-birth procedure. (Dr. Haskell called it "D&X," for dilation and extraction.)

Dr. Haskell brought the ultrasound in and hooked it up so that he could see the baby. On the ultrasound screen, I could see the heart beating. I asked Dr. Haskell, and he told me that, "Yes, that is the heartbeat." As Dr. Haskell watched the baby on the ultrasound screen, he went in with forceps and grabbed the baby's legs and brought them down into the birth canal. Then he delivered the body and arms, all the way up to the neck.

At this point, only the baby's head was still inside. The baby's body was moving. His little fingers were clasping together. He was kicking his feet. All the while his little head was still stuck inside. Dr Haskell took a pair of scissors and inserted them into the back of the baby's head. Then he opened the scissors up. Then he stuck the high-powered suction tube into the hole and sucked the baby's brains out. I almost threw up as I watched him do these things.

Next, Dr. Haskell delivered the baby's head, cut the umbilical cord and delivered the placenta. He threw the baby in a pan, along with the placenta and the instruments he'd used. I saw the baby move in the pan. I asked another nurse and she said it was just "reflexes."

The Fetus Is Alive

According to testimony presented to the Senate Judiciary Committee (November 17, 1995) [concerning the Partial-Birth Abortion Ban Act, H.R. 1833] by the American Society of Anesthesiologists, such claims [of fetal death due to anesthesia prior to a partial-birth abortion] have "absolutely no basis in scientific fact." The ASA says that regional anesthesia (used in many partial-birth abortions and most normal deliveries) has no effect on the fetus. General anesthesia has some sedating effect on the fetus, but much less than on the mother; even pain relief for the fetus is doubtful, and certainly anesthesia would not kill the baby, ASSA testified.

Douglas Johnson, *National Right to Life News*, November 30, 1995.

The woman wanted to see her baby, so they cleaned up the baby and put it in a blanket and handed the baby to her. She cried the whole time, and she kept saying, "I'm sorry, please forgive me." I was crying too. I couldn't take it. In all my professional years I had never experienced anything like this.

Another case I saw on that third day was a six-month-old (approximately 25 weeks) baby. The mother was over age 40. There was nothing wrong with this baby, she just didn't want it. The doctor used the same procedure, except he didn't use as much medicine to relax the lady as the first lady (who'd been very upset). This baby was also alive. I saw the heartbeat on the ultrasound. (Actually every baby that day still had a heartbeat at the time of the procedure.) The second baby was a little smaller than the first baby. I remember thinking how perfect this child was. This mother did not want to see it. The doctor didn't offer you this option, but if the mother insisted he let them see the baby. Otherwise he sent them back to a little room where another person examined them. A lab came and picked the babies up to dispose of them.

I also saw a third case that day. (I was only assisting in one operating room.) This was a 17-year-old girl. She was approximately 25 weeks. The same procedure was done on this baby.

Fetuses Are Babies

The Down's syndrome baby was the only baby that had a defect. And that baby with Down's syndrome had the most perfect, angelic face I have ever seen. I never realized how perfect these babies really are at this point. When you hear the word "fetus," I think a lot of people think as I did of just a blob of cells, or a mass of something. It was very revealing to me. I don't think about abortion the same way anymore. I still have nightmares about what I saw.

"[A late-term abortion] is sometimes the best of the rotten options."

Late-Term Abortion Should Not Be Banned

Ellen Goodman

Late-term (or partial-birth) abortion refers to those abortions that are performed after 24 weeks of pregnancy. In the following viewpoint, Ellen Goodman, a syndicated newspaper columnist, argues that this procedure is most commonly performed when tests have revealed serious defects in the fetus or the woman's health is at risk. Late-term abortion should not be banned because it is often the only realistic option in tragic medical circumstances, Goodman maintains. Furthermore, she contends, banning late-term abortion is just the first step toward criminalizing all abortions.

As you read, consider the following questions:

1. Why are the anti-abortion lobby's tactics against late-term abortions clever and malicious, in Goodman's opinion?
2. What is misleading about the anti-abortion lobby's argument against late-term abortions, according to the author?
3. Why should late-term abortions be allowed in order to protect a woman's health, in Goodman's opinion?

Ellen Goodman, "Painting the Whole Picture of Late-Term Abortions," *Liberal Opinion Week*, November 20, 1995; ©1995, The Boston Globe Newspaper Co./ Washington Post Writers Group. Reprinted with permission.

In the drawings all you see of the woman is a womb.

The black-and-white sketches that have become truly *graphic art* for the debate over late-term abortions don't show the shock on Vikki Stella's face when a routine pregnancy became "Oh, my God."

They don't show Tammy Watts' expression when the doctor reading her ultrasound said quietly, "There is something I did not expect to see."

Nor do they show Coreen Costello's pain when she discovered that there was something horribly wrong with the child she was expecting and that the amniotic fluid puddled in her uterus could rupture at any time.

The woman, her family and her humanity have been cropped out of the illustrations shown on the Senate floor as if they were irrelevant.

As for the fetus in this pro-life portfolio, the perfect, Gerber-baby outline of a fetus in the birth canal? It doesn't look much like the one in Viki Wilson's sonogram, with two-thirds of her brain lodged in a separate sack, looking "as if she had two heads." Nor does it look like the Watts' fetus which had no eyes, six fingers and six toes and a mass of bowel and bladder outside of her stomach.

Would full-color, real-life illustrations be too graphic for legislators? Would it have been too sensational to show torn cervixes on television, fetuses for whom the decision wasn't life or death, but what kind of death? Or are they too vivid a portrait of the real tragedies that force families and doctors into painful decisions.

"Partial-Birth Abortions"

Over the past months, we have watched the phrase "partial-birth abortion" forced into the political language by sheer repetition.

It's been used over and again to mislabel a rarely used medical technique called "intact dilation and evacuation."

A bill [the Partial-Birth Abortion Ban Act (HR1833)] to criminalize this procedure—described with inflammatory inaccuracy as the scissor-stabbing murder of a conscious baby—sailed through the House. It barely lost momentum in the Senate and was temporarily detoured to the judiciary committee.

But when the hearings begin next Friday (November 17, 1995), the chamber will once again be turned into an anti-abortion art gallery. [The bill passed both houses in 1995 but was vetoed by Bill Clinton in April 1996.]

What is clever about this new visual tack of the anti-abortion leaders is that any late-term abortion is gruesome. What is malicious about this attack is that it's aimed at families that wanted babies, at women whose pregnancies went terribly awry.

A reckless Maureen Malloy of the National Right to Life Committee, described "healthy women carrying healthy babies." An overheated Bob Smith, the Republican senator from New Hampshire, waxing on about the trip through the birth canal, called the doctor "an executioner."

They talked as if women carried their pregnancies for 36 weeks and then decided, "oops, I changed my mind." As if doctors performed such treatments "on demand."

Chipping Away at a Woman's Rights

Legislation . . . to ban late-term abortion procedures will once again jeopardize a woman's right to choose the outcome of her life. A minute percentage of abortions take place in the third trimester, and these occur only when the woman is in danger of losing her life or there are severe anomalies in the fetus. Chip away at the right to choose an abortion and sooner than we think, women . . . will have no safe options available. Fewer doctors are willing to risk their lives to serve women's health clinics and with good reason: Terrorist activities have paralyzed places that used to be safe havens for women for whom pregnancy was not desirable or sustainable. This legislation will embolden anti-choice activists in their relentless efforts to overturn *Roe vs. Wade*.

Shira Stern, *Los Angeles Times*, October 30, 1995.

If you only saw these drawings on the board, you would not know that state laws already restrict late-term abortions except for the life or health of the woman. Nor would you know that this procedure is sometimes the best of the rotten options—the one that may best enable a woman to have another baby. You wouldn't even know that anesthesia ends the life of such a fetus before it comes down the birth canal.

But this artwork is just the most recent rendering of the anti-abortion strategy. For years, they have targeted doctors, the "weak link" of abortion rights, through harassment, death threats, violence. Now they are threatening them with jail.

The First Step

For the first time, Congress has been asked to outlaw a medical procedure. If it works, right-to-life advocates hope to eliminate abortion, one procedure and one prosecution at a time.

Under the current bill, doctors who don't practice the congressionally approved protocol risk two years in prison. Even if the Senate amends the law to permit this technique to save the life of a woman, it would not be allowed to "merely" save her health. What would that mean? A legislated ruptured uterus? A

portant interest in potential life, and are overruled. This is clear even on the very terms of *Akron I* and *Thornburgh*. Those decisions, along with *Planned Parenthood of Central Missouri v. Danforth*, 1976, recognize a substantial government interest justifying a requirement that a woman be apprised of the health risks of abortion and childbirth. It cannot be questioned that psychological well-being is a facet of health. Nor can it be doubted that most women considering an abortion would deem the impact on the fetus relevant, if not dispositive, to the decision. In attempting to ensure that a woman apprehend the full consequences of her decision, the State furthers the legitimate purpose of reducing the risk that a woman may elect an abortion, only to discover later, with devastating psychological consequences, that her decision was not fully informed. If the information the State requires to be made available to the woman is truthful and not misleading, the requirement may be permissible.

A Reasonable Measure

We also see no reason why the State may not require doctors to inform a woman seeking an abortion of the availability of materials relating to the consequences to the fetus, even when those consequences have no direct relation to her health. An example illustrates the point. We would think it constitutional for the State to require that in order for there to be informed consent to a kidney transplant operation the recipient must be supplied with information about risks to the donor as well as risks to himself or herself. A requirement that the physician make available information similar to that mandated by the statute here was described in *Thornburgh* as "an outright attempt to wedge the Commonwealth's message discouraging abortion into the privacy of the informed-consent dialogue between the woman and her physician." We conclude, however, that informed choice need not be defined in such narrow terms that all considerations of the effect on the fetus are made irrelevant. As we have made clear, we depart from the holdings of *Akron I* and *Thornburgh* to the extent that we permit a State to further its legitimate goal of protecting the life of the unborn by enacting legislation aimed at ensuring a decision that is mature and informed, even when in so doing the State expresses a preference for childbirth over abortion. In short, requiring that the woman be informed of the availability of information relating to fetal development and the assistance available should she decide to carry the pregnancy to full term is a reasonable measure to ensure an informed choice, one which might cause the woman to choose childbirth over abortion. This requirement cannot be considered a substantial obstacle to obtaining an abortion, and, it follows, there is no undue burden. . . .

"mere" hemorrhage? Who would decide?

Senator Barbara Boxer, a mother and grandmother, spoke to her colleagues last week and asked these senators to, yes, think about "babies." She asked them to think of their own babies, growing and grown daughters, whose futures could be at risk.

Now the hearing room is set to become a "drawing room." Stark black-and-white renderings of womb and fetus will carry all the easy appeal of propaganda into the judiciary committee.

But life doesn't always imitate art. And in this real world, only the women whose pregnancies turned into "Oh, my God" can paint the whole picture.

5

"The idea that important decisions will be more informed and deliberate if they follow some period of reflection does not strike us as unreasonable."

A 24-Hour Waiting Period Is Not an Undue Burden

Sandra Day O'Connor, Anthony Kennedy, and David Souter

Sandra Day O'Connor, Anthony Kennedy, and David Souter are U.S. Supreme Court justices and authors of the joint opinion in *Planned Parenthood of Southeastern Pennsylvania v. Casey*, from which this viewpoint is excerpted. The justices argue that imposing a mandatory 24-hour waiting period in which a woman may reflect on her decision does not constitute a substantial obstacle to abortion. Requiring a pregnant woman to be informed of the risks of and alternatives to abortion is permitted under the *Roe v. Wade* decision and does not violate a woman's constitutional rights, they maintain.

As you read, consider the following questions:

1. According to the justices, how did the *Akron I* and *Thornburgh* decisions go too far in the matter of informed consent?
2. What reasons did the Supreme Court justices give for changing their decision in *Akron I* concerning the Pennsylvania statute's requirement for a 24-hour waiting period?
3. What is the right protected by the U.S. Supreme Court decision in *Roe v. Wade*, according to O'Connor, Kennedy, and Souter?

From Sandra Day O'Connor, Anthony Kennedy, and David Souter, *Planned Parenthood of Southeastern Pennsylvania v. Robert P. Casey*, 112 Sup. Ct. 2791 (1992).

The informed consent requirement of the Pennsylvania Abortion Control Act of 1982 . . . requires that at least 24 hours before performing an abortion a physician inform the woman of the nature of the procedure, the health risks of the abortion and of childbirth, and the "probable gestational age of the unborn child." The physician or a qualified nonphysician must inform the woman of the availability of printed materials published by the State describing the fetus and providing information about medical assistance for childbirth, information about child support from the father, and a list of agencies which provide adoption and other services as alternatives to abortion. An abortion may not be performed unless the woman certifies in writing that she has been informed of the availability of these printed materials and has been provided them if she chooses to view them.

Our prior decisions establish that as with any medical procedure, the State may require a woman to give her written informed consent to an abortion. In this respect, the Pennsylvania statute is unexceptional. Petitioners challenge the statute's definition of informed consent because it includes the provision of specific information by the doctor and the mandatory 24-hour waiting period. The conclusions reached by a majority of the Supreme Court Justices in the separate opinions filed today and the undue burden standard adopted in this opinion require us to overrule in part some of the Supreme Court's past decisions, decisions driven by the trimester framework's prohibition of previability regulations designed to further the State's interest in fetal life.

Constitutional and Unconstitutional Requirements

In the 1983 decision in *Akron (Ohio) v. Akron Center for Reproductive Health, Inc. (Akron I)*, we invalidated an ordinance which required that a woman seeking an abortion be provided by her physician with specific information "designed to influence the woman's informed choice between abortion or childbirth." As we later described the *Akron I* holding in *Thornburgh v. American College of Obstetricians and Gynecologists*, 1986, there were two purported flaws in the Akron ordinance: the information was designed to dissuade the woman from having an abortion and the ordinance imposed "a rigid requirement that a specific body of information be given in all cases, irrespective of the particular needs of the patient."

To the extent *Akron I* and *Thornburgh* find a constitutional violation when the government requires, as it does here, the giving of truthful, nonmisleading information about the nature of the procedure, the attendant health risks and those of childbirth, and the "probable gestational age" of the fetus, those cases go too far, are inconsistent with *Roe v. Wade*'s acknowledgment of an

Our analysis of Pennsylvania's 24-hour waiting period between the provision of the information deemed necessary to informed consent and the performance of an abortion under the undue burden standard requires us to reconsider the premise behind the decision in *Akron I* invalidating a parallel requirement. In *Akron I* we said: "Nor are we convinced that the State's legitimate concern that the woman's decision be informed is reasonably served by requiring a 24-hour delay as a matter of course." We consider that conclusion to be wrong. The idea that important decisions will be more informed and deliberate if they follow some period of reflection does not strike us as unreasonable, particularly where the statute directs that important information become part of the background of the decision. The statute, as construed by the Court of Appeals, permits avoidance of the waiting period in the event of a medical emergency and the record evidence shows that in the vast majority of cases, a 24-hour delay does not create any appreciable health risk. In theory, at least, the waiting period is a reasonable measure to implement the State's interest in protecting the life of the unborn, a measure that does not amount to an undue burden.

Why Is a Delay Bad?

Planned Parenthood [argues that] informed consent legislation . . . may delay an abortion or prevent a woman from obtaining one altogether. The threshold question is whether either of these outcomes is inherently bad and why. From a health standpoint, informed consent legislation is usually tied to a requirement that 24 hours transpire between the dissemination of information to a woman regarding abortion and the actual procedure. While differences in the safety of abortion at various stages of pregnancy, and by method used, are anything but negligible, the medical significance of a single day's delay is not considerable.

Charles A. Donovan, *Family Policy*, October 1993.

Whether the mandatory 24-hour waiting period is nonetheless invalid because in practice it is a substantial obstacle to a woman's choice to terminate her pregnancy is a closer question. The findings of fact by the District Court indicate that because of the distances many women must travel to reach an abortion provider, the practical effect will often be a delay of much more than a day because the waiting period requires that a woman seeking an abortion make at least two visits to the doctor. The District Court also found that in many instances this will increase the exposure of women seeking abortions to "the harassment and hostility of anti-abortion protestors demonstrating outside a clinic." As a result, the District Court found that for those women who have the fewest financial resources, those who must travel long distances, and those who have difficulty explaining their whereabouts to husbands, employers, or others, the 24-hour waiting period will be "particularly burdensome."

Not an Undue Burden

These findings are troubling in some respects, but they do not demonstrate that the waiting period constitutes an undue burden. We do not doubt that, as the District Court held, the waiting period has the effect of "increasing the cost and risk of delay of abortions," but the District Court did not conclude that the increased costs and potential delays amount to substantial obstacles. Rather, applying the trimester framework's strict prohibition of all regulation designed to promote the State's interest in potential life before viability, the District Court concluded that the waiting period does not further the state's "interest in maternal health" and "infringes the physician's discretion to exercise sound medical judgment." Yet, as we have stated, under the undue burden standard a State is permitted to enact persuasive measures which favor childbirth over abortion, even if those measures do not further a health interest. And while the waiting period does limit a physician's discretion, that is not, standing alone, a reason to invalidate it. In light of the construction given the statute's definition of medical emergency by the Court of Appeals, and the District Court's findings, we cannot say that the waiting period imposes a real health risk.

We also disagree with the District Court's conclusion that the "particularly burdensome" effects of the waiting period on some women require its invalidation. A particular burden is not of necessity a substantial obstacle. Whether a burden falls on a particular group is a distinct inquiry from whether it is a substantial obstacle even as to the women in that group. And the District Court did not conclude that the waiting period is such an obstacle even for the women who are most burdened by it. . . .

We are left with the argument that the various aspects of the informed consent requirement are unconstitutional because they place barriers in the way of abortion on demand. Even the broadest reading of *Roe*, however, has not suggested that there is a constitutional right to abortion on demand. Rather, the right protected by *Roe* is a right to decide to terminate a pregnancy free of undue interference by the State. Because the informed consent requirement facilitates the wise exercise of that right it cannot be classified as an interference with the right *Roe* protects. The informed consent requirement is not an undue burden on that right.

> *"A woman who has . . . made her decision cannot be forced to reconsider all, simply because the State believes she has come to the wrong conclusion."*

A 24-Hour Waiting Period Is an Undue Burden

John Paul Stevens

The following viewpoint is taken from the dissenting opinion of John Paul Stevens, a Supreme Court justice, in the case *Planned Parenthood of Southeastern Pennsylvania v. Casey*, in which the Supreme Court allowed states to require informed consent and a mandatory 24-hour waiting period for a woman seeking an abortion. A state may prefer that women choose to give birth rather than to abort, Stevens contends, but it is unconstitutional for the state to attempt to influence women's decisions by requiring doctors to present prejudicial information. The 24-hour waiting period constitutes an undue burden for women and therefore should not be permitted, he maintains.

As you read, consider the following questions:

1. Why are the arguments that a 24-hour waiting period furthers the state's interests invalid, according to Stevens?
2. What makes a state-imposed burden on the exercise of a constitutional right an "undue" burden, in the author's opinion?
3. According to the author, why are the informational requirements of the Pennsylvania statute of little value to most women making a decision to abort?

From John Paul Stevens, *Planned Parenthood of Southeastern Pennsylvania v. Robert P. Casey*, 112 Sup. Ct. 2791 (1992).

The U.S. Supreme Court recognized in the *Thornburgh v. American College of Obstetricians and Gynecologists* decision that a woman considering abortion faces "a difficult choice having serious and personal consequences of major importance to her own future—perhaps to the salvation of her own immortal soul." The authority to make such traumatic and yet empowering decisions is an element of basic human dignity. As the Supreme Court's joint opinion so eloquently demonstrates, a woman's decision to terminate her pregnancy is nothing less than a matter of conscience.

The State's Interests Versus Individual Freedoms

Weighing the State's interest in potential life and the woman's liberty interest, I agree with the joint opinion that the State may "expres[s] a preference for normal childbirth," that the State may take steps to ensure that a woman's choice "is thoughtful and informed," and that "States are free to enact laws to provide a reasonable framework for a woman to make a decision that has such profound and lasting meaning." Serious questions arise, however, when a State attempts to "persuade the woman to choose childbirth over abortion." Decisional autonomy must limit the State's power to inject into a woman's most personal deliberations its own views of what is best. The State may promote its preferences by funding childbirth, by creating and maintaining alternatives to abortion, and by espousing the virtues of family; but it must respect the individual's freedom to make such judgments.

This theme runs throughout the Supreme Court's decisions concerning reproductive freedom. In general, *Roe v. Wade*'s requirement that restrictions on abortions before viability be justified by the State's interest in maternal health has prevented States from interjecting regulations designed to influence a woman's decision. Thus, we have upheld regulations of abortion that are not efforts to sway or direct a woman's choice but rather are efforts to enhance the deliberative quality of that decision or are neutral regulations on the health aspects of her decision. We have, for example, upheld regulations requiring written informed consent, limited recordkeeping and reporting, and pathology reports, as well as various licensing and qualification provisions. Conversely, we have consistently rejected State efforts to prejudice a woman's choice, either by limiting the information available to her, or, as we stated in *Thornburgh*, by "requir[ing] the delivery of information designed 'to influence the woman's informed choice between abortion or childbirth.'"

In my opinion, the principles established in this long line of cases and the wisdom reflected in Justice Lewis Powell's 1983 opinion for the Court in *Akron (Ohio) v. Akron Center for Repro-*

ductive Health, Inc. (and followed by the Court in *Thornburgh*) should govern our decision today. Under these principles, sections 3205(a) (2) (i)–(iii) of the Pennsylvania Abortion Control Act of 1982 are unconstitutional. Those sections require a physician or counselor to provide the woman with a range of materials clearly designed to persuade her to choose not to undergo the abortion. While the State is free, pursuant to section 3208 of the Pennsylvania law, to produce and disseminate such material, the State may not inject such information into the woman's deliberations just as she is weighing such an important choice.

Reprinted by permission of Signe Wilkinson and Cartoonists & Writers Syndicate.

Under this same analysis, section 3205(a) (1) (i) and (iii) of the Pennsylvania statute are constitutional. Those sections, which require the physician to inform a woman of the nature and risks of the abortion procedure and the medical risks of carrying to term, are neutral requirements comparable to those imposed in other medical procedures. Those sections indicate no effort by the State to influence the woman's choice in any way. If anything, such requirements enhance, rather than skew, the woman's decisionmaking.

The 24-Hour Waiting Period

The 24-hour waiting period required by the Pennsylvania statute raises even more serious concerns. Such a requirement arguably furthers the State's interests in two ways, neither of which is constitutionally permissible.

First, it may be argued that the 24-hour delay is justified by the mere fact that it is likely to reduce the number of abortions, thus furthering the State's interest in potential life. But such an argument would justify any form of coercion that placed an obstacle in the woman's path. The State cannot further its interests by simply wearing down the ability of the pregnant woman to exercise her constitutional right.

Second, it can more reasonably be argued that the 24-hour delay furthers the State's interest in ensuring that the woman's decision is informed and thoughtful. But there is no evidence that the mandated delay benefits women or that it is necessary to enable the physician to convey any relevant information to the patient. The mandatory delay thus appears to rest on outmoded and unacceptable assumptions about the decisionmaking capacity of women. While there are well-established and consistently maintained reasons for the State to view with skepticism the ability of minors to make decisions, none of those reasons applies to an adult woman's decisionmaking ability. Just as we have left behind the belief that a woman must consult her husband before undertaking serious matters, so we must reject the notion that a woman is less capable of deciding matters of gravity.

In the alternative, the delay requirement may be premised on the belief that the decision to terminate a pregnancy is presumptively wrong. This premise is illegitimate. Those who disagree vehemently about the legality and morality of abortion agree about one thing: The decision to terminate a pregnancy is profound and difficult. No person undertakes such a decision lightly—and States may not presume that a woman has failed to reflect adequately merely because her conclusion differs from the State's preference. A woman who has, in the privacy of her thoughts and conscience, weighed the options and made her decision cannot be forced to reconsider all, simply because the State believes she has come to the wrong conclusion.

Part of the constitutional liberty to choose is the equal dignity to which each of us is entitled. A woman who decides to terminate her pregnancy is entitled to the same respect as a woman who decides to carry the fetus to term. The mandatory waiting period denies women that equal respect.

An Undue Burden

In my opinion, a correct application of the "undue burden" standard leads to the same conclusion concerning the constitutionality of these requirements. A state-imposed burden on the exercise of a constitutional right is measured both by its effects and by its character: A burden may be "undue" either because the burden is too severe or because it lacks a legitimate, rational justification.

The 24-hour delay requirement fails both parts of this test. The findings of the District Court establish the severity of the burden that the 24-hour delay imposes on many pregnant women. Yet even in those cases in which the delay is not especially onerous, it is, in my opinion, "undue" because there is no evidence that such a delay serves a useful and legitimate purpose. As indicated above, there is no legitimate reason to require a woman who has agonized over her decision to leave the clinic or hospital and return again another day. While a general requirement that a physician notify her patients about the risks of a proposed medical procedure is appropriate, a rigid requirement that all patients wait 24 hours or (what is true in practice) much longer to evaluate the significance of information that is either common knowledge or irrelevant is an irrational and, therefore, "undue" burden.

The counseling provisions are similarly infirm. Whenever government commands private citizens to speak or to listen, careful review of the justification for that command is particularly appropriate. In this case, the Pennsylvania statute directs that counselors provide women seeking abortions with information concerning alternatives to abortion, the availability of medical assistance benefits, and the possibility of child-support payments. The statute requires that this information be given to all women seeking abortions, including those for whom such information is clearly useless, such as those who are married, those who have undergone the procedure in the past and are fully aware of the options, and those who are fully convinced that abortion is their only reasonable option. Moreover, the statute requires physicians to inform all of their patients of "the probable gestational age of the unborn child." This information is of little decisional value in most cases, because 90 percent of all abortions are performed during the first trimester when fetal age has less relevance than when the fetus nears viability. Nor can the information required by the statute be justified as relevant to any "philosophic" or "social" argument, either favoring or disfavoring the abortion decision in a particular case. In light of all of these facts, I conclude that the information requirements of the Pennsylvania statute do not serve a useful purpose and thus constitute an unnecessary—and therefore undue—burden on the woman's constitutional liberty to decide to terminate her pregnancy.

"School officials are not allowed to hand out aspirin for headaches without parental consent. . . . The same should apply with abortions."

Parental Consent Laws Are Necessary

Adrienne T. Washington

In the following viewpoint, Adrienne T. Washington argues that parental consent laws, which require the notification or consent of a teenager's parents before the teenager can have an abortion, are necessary. Parents are legally responsible for their teenagers and therefore have a right to know if their daughter is planning to have an abortion, Washington contends. No other medical procedure can be performed on a teenager without a parent's knowledge and consent, she asserts, and abortion should be no different. Washington is a columnist for the *Washington Times*.

As you read, consider the following questions:

1. At what age would a teenager become exempt from the proposed parental notification law, according to the author?
2. How would parental notification laws act as a deterrent to teenage sex, according to Brandi Berry, as cited by Washington?
3. When should judges be allowed to waive the parental notification law, in the author's opinion?

Adrienne T. Washington, "Ask a Kid: Parents Need Abortion Notice," *Washington Times*, March 11, 1994. Reprinted by permission of the *Washington Times*, ©1994.

Brandi Berry had no idea what "parental notification" meant. The idea was so foreign to the 14-year-old District of Columbia honor student that she first needed a primer on the controversial issue before she could give her thoughts about it.

Parental Rights and Responsibilities

You see, Brandi lives in a home with consistent, unwavering rules. She and her two sisters know exactly what is expected of them. Their parents, Reginald and Frances, have left no doubt that there will be swift and harsh punishment for disobedience—and rewards for excellence.

"From the time I can remember, I've been taught that I'm not officially an adult until I'm 18 and any decisions affecting me will be decided by my parents until then," she says emphatically.

Even then, some important decisions affecting her future will be made by her parents until she is 21 years old. No problem.

So Brandi, who understands the role "family values" play in her life, really can't comprehend how a teen-ager can obtain an abortion without her parents' knowledge.

"It's the parents' responsibility to know everything else, especially when it's a medical problem involved, so they should know about this too," Brandi says.

I consulted with Brandi on parental notification because the Virginia General Assembly continues to wrestle with the politically charged issue.

The [state] Senate has repeatedly refused to pass a bill requiring a physician to notify at least one parent before performing an abortion on a girl who is 17 or younger. A judge would be able to waive the requirement with a determination that the girl was "mature enough" or endangered by parental notification.

Gov. George Allen may still prevail upon the legislature to pass the measure before adjourning March 12, 1994. [The bill was carried over to the 1995 session where it failed in committee.] He intends to, and he should. An overwhelming majority of Virginians agree with him.

This issue is more about parental rights than abortion rights.

But what do you expect from adults? I wanted a young person's perspective, so I asked my young friend Brandi, who is a quick-witted, straightforward kind of girl.

In fact, Brandi is a colleague of sorts. She also writes an opinion column. "Brandi's Corner" appears in the *Washington Afro-American* about twice a month, depending on her demanding schedule. I met her at a taping of a NewsChannel 8 special on Black History Month, which featured her artistic and academic accomplishments.

Brandi believes that if parental notification laws were enacted they could be used as deterrents to keep young women from getting pregnant.

"Hey, if people know they can get pregnant and have an abortion and not have their parents find out, then what's to stop them?" she asks.

Brandi knows full well the consequences she would face in such a predicament.

"I know my father, and I know what he'll do. If I ever got pregnant, I know that my behind would be in the street or at some other relative's house," she says.

Parental Responsibility

Mrs. Judie Brown, president of the American Life League in Stafford, Virginia, says we must support "the idea of notifying parents in advance when any kind of discussion goes on with regard to their children's health and welfare, and that includes abortion. As long as parents are responsible for their children, they should certainly be responsible for their sexuality." She expresses support also for parental notification laws, observing: "Laws are written to stipulate what is right and wrong. And when it comes to a law that affects parental rights, I think there is a responsibility to come out on the side of the parents."

Haven Bradford Gow, *Conservative Review*, September/October 1995.

Besides her father's strict stance, her mother repeatedly drills, "No boys, no condoms, no sex."

"My mother says boys are not schoolwork, and you have to be about your schoolwork. . . . Boys can't give you A's and B's and you have to get A's and B's," Brandi says. "So I'm busting those A's and I'm happy."

A Legal Right

If only more youngsters had the benefit of such obviously good parenting as Brandi has. But good parents should not be legally barred from doing their jobs.

Parental notification is one of those troubling topics that confound many. While I believe in a woman's right to choose what's in her best interest, I am also a parent.

Abortion is a different story when it comes to an impressionable and vulnerable teen-age girl. She is still someone's child. She is still some adult's legal, financial and moral responsibility.

As young Brandi says, "How will the parents feel if something happens and they didn't even know about it?"

My offspring are young adults now, but when they were younger I would have raised a ruckus had anyone performed any medical procedures on them without my knowledge. Simple as that.

Who wouldn't, unless you're the type of parent or adult who's abdicated your responsibilities with regard to your children? Abusers and absconders come to mind here. That's when judges should be brought in.

But in the case of most children, school officials are not allowed to hand out aspirin for headaches without parental consent. If your child winds up in a hospital emergency room with a broken arm or leg, no one can touch the child until you arrive or grant your authority for treatment over the telephone.

The same should apply with abortions.

Don't just take an old fuddy-duddy's word for it. Ask a 14-year-old sage like Brandi Berry who's glad to have her parents making decisions for her. At least until she's 21.

"[Parental consent laws] hurt rather than help many teens."

Parental Consent Laws Are Harmful to Teens

Jennifer Coburn

Many states have enacted legislation that requires teenagers seeking an abortion to notify their parents of their decision or to obtain their consent. These laws are unconstitutional and can be detrimental to the life and well-being of pregnant teenagers, argues Jennifer Coburn in the following viewpoint. For instance, parental consent laws threaten the health of girls who have illegal abortions in order to avoid telling their parents, Coburn maintains. Most teens talk voluntarily to one or both parents about their decision to have an abortion, she contends, and those who do not usually have a very good reason. Coburn is the public affairs coordinator at Planned Parenthood of San Diego and Riverside Counties and the former president of the San Diego chapter of the National Organization for Women.

As you read, consider the following questions:

1. According to the Alan Guttmacher Institute, as cited by Coburn, what percentage of teens talk to their parents about their decision to have an abortion?
2. Why are parental consent laws unconstitutional, according to the author?
3. How do parental consent laws fit in with the long-term strategy of abortion opponents, in Coburn's opinion?

Jennifer Coburn, "Parental Consent Puts Teens in a Bind," *San Diego Union-Tribune*, January 10, 1996. Reprinted by permission of the author.

On January 10, 1996, the California Supreme Court is scheduled to hear oral arguments in *American Academy of Pediatrics vs. Lungren*, a case which may secure or curtail a young woman's right to choose abortion in our state. The case could either uphold or reverse a Superior Court injunction blocking the parental-consent law championed by San Diego Assemblyman Bob Frazee in 1987. [In April 1996 the California Supreme Court ruled that this parental-consent law is constitutional.]

When most people hear about parental-consent laws, they find them pretty reasonable. After all, parents want to know what their children are doing so they can offer guidance and support. This is especially true when discussing important issues such as pregnancy and abortion.

The fact is that most teens voluntarily involve parents in this intensely personal decision. The Alan Guttmacher Institute reports that 60 percent of young women in the United States seek input from their parents when considering terminating a pregnancy. This is without the government legislating family communication. The 40 percent who do not involve parents usually have very good reasons for their decision.

Laws that Hurt Teens

Many people who support parental consent to abortion laws do so out of genuine concern for young people. But a closer look at these laws reveals that they hurt rather than help many teens.

Teens who do not seek parental guidance are often physically and emotionally abused, or victims of incest. The story of a 13-year-old from Idaho is one of the many laced with tragedy. Impregnated by her father, this sixth-grader scheduled an abortion in a neighboring state with her mother's assistance. After learning of his daughter's intention to terminate the pregnancy, he fatally shot her.

In 1988, an Indiana high school senior died from a botched illegal abortion in an attempt to circumvent the state's parental-consent law. Although the state had judicial bypass—which would allow her to beg the court's permission in lieu of her parents'—the girl knew the judge who would hear her case was notorious for denying abortion rights to minors.

Not wanting to disappoint her parents, she did not tell them and sought an illegal abortion. She sacrificed safety for privacy and paid the ultimate price.

The Indiana girl's parents originally supported their state's parental-consent law because they believed it would strengthen families. Today, they speak out against the policy they believed killed their daughter.

Legislators who oppose abortion believe that parental-consent laws will scare teens into abstinence. However, in states with these laws, sexual activity rates do not decrease. All that increases are health risks. Young people are frightened by these laws, but only after they are pregnant and desperately seeking help.

Not only does the California parental-consent law jeopardize the safety of young people, it is wholly unconstitutional. The U.S. Supreme Court legalized abortion in 1973, based on the constitutional right to privacy. Nowhere is that right qualified by age of the citizen.

A Disaster for Teens

There is evidence that teenagers who do not involve their parents [in deciding about abortion] believe that involving their parents would not be in their own best interests or are trying to protect their parents.

While telling parents is never easy, for some it could be a disaster. When teenagers in Minnesota were asked why they feared to tell their parents, the reasons included parents' physical or psychiatric illness; parents' drug or alcohol abuse; and the probability of verbal, physical, or sexual abuse. Some even said they had never met the parent.

According to the federal district court that examined the effects of Minnesota's parental notification statute, "Notification of the minor's pregnancy and abortion decision can provoke violence, even where the parents are divorced or separated."

Planned Parenthood Federation of America, Inc., *Teenagers, Abortion, and Government Intrusion Laws*, 1992.

Further, if the California Supreme Court reverses the lower-court decision, it will essentially establish that young people are the property of their parents. If parents can prohibit a daughter's abortion, what's stopping them from forcing one?

If it's perfectly legal for parents to decide their daughters must not terminate a pregnancy, the court must also uphold a "parent's right" to insist she does. Under this law, parents would own the bodies of their children. Would we then see perpetrators of incest and abuse citing the flawed decision in defense of their deplorable actions?

Abortion-rights advocates wish to preserve minors' access to confidential reproductive health services, including abortion, because it protects the health and safety of young people. While parental involvement is strongly encouraged in contraception and abortion decisions, supporters of legal abortion know that the government cannot mandate healthy communication.

Chipping Away at the Right to Choose

Opponents of abortion view parental-consent laws as part of a long-term strategy to make abortion—under any circumstance—illegal. Parental-consent laws, waiting periods and funding rollbacks are all part of their legislative effort to chip away at the right to choose.

Coupled with the terrorist tactics of extremists who bomb clinics, harass patients and shoot doctors, access to services is seriously threatened. And without access, the right to choose is meaningless.

In making its decision, the California Supreme Court must decide if minors are protected by the same constitutional right to privacy as adults, or if their safety will be sacrificed to promote the political agenda of the far right. If the court thoroughly examines the effect of mandated parental consent in other states, it will see that these laws sustain abortion rights in name only.

Periodical Bibliography

The following articles have been selected to supplement the diverse views presented in this chapter. Addresses are provided for periodicals not indexed in the *Readers' Guide to Periodical Literature*, the *Alternative Press Index*, or the *Social Sciences Index*.

American Medical Association Council on Ethical and Judicial Affairs — "Mandatory Parental Consent to Abortion," *JAMA*, January 6, 1993. Available from Subscriber Services Center, American Medical Association, 515 N. State St., Chicago, IL 60610.

Hadley Arkes — "The Eight-Week Solution," *Crisis*, March 1994. Available from PO Box 1006, Notre Dame, IN 46556.

Hadley Arkes — "German Judges and Undue Burdens," *Crisis*, July/August 1994.

Janet Benshoof — *"Planned Parenthood v. Casey,"* *JAMA*, May 5, 1993.

George J. Church — "Pro-Life and Pro-Choice? Yes!" *Time*, March 6, 1995.

Marc Cooper — "The Changing Landscape of Abortion," *Glamour*, August 1995.

Norine Dworkin — "The Abortion Issue: There Is No 'Choice' Without Providers," *On the Issues*, Fall 1993. Available from PO Box 3000, Dept. OTI, Denville, NJ 07834.

Ellen Goodman — "Pro-Life Vigilantism," *Liberal Opinion Week*, October 9, 1995. Available from PO Box 468, Vinton, IA 52349.

James L. Graff — "Calling the Cops on a Pregnant Girlfriend," *Time*, October 9, 1995.

Steven R. Hemler, Richard G. Wilkins, and Frank H. Fischer — "Abortion: A Principled Politics," *National Review*, December 27, 1993.

Lisa Leiter and Chi Chi Sileo — "Antiabortion Lawmakers Try to Redefine the Fourteenth," *Insight*, December 18, 1995. Available from 3600 New York Ave. NE, Washington, DC 20002.

Frederica Mathewes-Green — "Embryonic Trend: How Do We Explain the Drop in Abortions?" *Policy Review*, Summer 1995.

Alissa Rubin — "Partial Truths," *New Republic*, March 4, 1996.

3 CHAPTER

Can Abortion Be Justified?

Abortion

Chapter Preface

Almost 60 percent of all pregnancies in the United States are unintended at the time of conception, according to a 1995 report released by the Institute of Medicine (IOM). The report further states that each year 25 percent of all U.S. pregnancies—many of which are a result of birth control failure—end in abortion.

A 1994 Roper poll found that while 55 percent of Americans approve of abortion in the hard cases—for rape, incest, fetal deformity, or when the life or health of the mother is threatened—only 37 percent support the use of abortion to end an unwanted pregnancy. Many Americans believe that having an abortion because an unwanted child would disrupt the woman's life is equivalent to using abortion as birth control, a practice they condemn as selfish and immoral.

According to family planning advocates, however, most women do not use abortion as a birth control method. Typically, a woman has 30 or more fertile years, which translates to about 400 chances to get pregnant during her lifetime. Therefore, abortion rights activists maintain, it should not be considered unusual for a woman to make a mistake or experience birth control failure at least once during those years. In such a case, they argue, it is less selfish for a woman to choose to abort an unwanted pregnancy than to have an unwanted, unloved, and uncared-for child.

Abortions in cases of rape and fetal deformity may be defended more easily than abortions in the case of an unwanted pregnancy, but the arguments involved are no less intense. The authors in the following chapter debate whether any reason is good enough to justify abortion.

"Not wanting a child strongly is the best possible reason to have an abortion."

An Unwanted Pregnancy Justifies an Abortion

Patricia Lunneborg

The majority of women who have abortions do so because their contraception fails and the resulting pregnancy is unwanted, contends Patricia Lunneborg in the following viewpoint. Although many Americans disapprove of abortions for reasons other than rape, incest, or preserving a pregnant woman's health, Lunneborg argues, an unwanted pregnancy is actually a valid reason for having an abortion. She maintains that many women are unable to take responsibility for raising a child at the time they become pregnant and that abortion is therefore an appropriate option for them. Lunneborg, a retired professor of psychology and adjunct professor of women's studies at the University of Washington in Seattle, is the author of *Abortion: A Positive Decision*, from which this viewpoint is excerpted.

As you read, consider the following questions:

1. How often do condoms leak during intercourse, as cited by the author?
2. What are the top six reasons women give for having an abortion, according to Lunneborg?
3. According to Lunneborg, what are the three choices a woman faces when she is pregnant?

A vibrant, forward-looking, 35-year-old abortion clinic super-visor, who personally has not made the abortion decision, said this about it.

The abortion decision comes from your whole life and how you think about yourself, not just the circumstances of the present time. I feel it's important for women to acknowledge that sometimes they have got a choice, even though it's not a very good one. Like living on welfare, it is a choice, even though it's not attractive. But you acknowledge that people have got a choice, even if it is a very small amount of choice because of their circumstances, but they must make that choice for themselves. Because I feel if that doesn't happen, then you're going to have problems afterwards. For abortion or anything.

Women may say, Oh, I don't want to have a baby because I haven't enough money, or my partner and I haven't known one another very long. When I feel it's good just to say, I don't want a baby at the moment. I think that's perfectly all right. There's nothing stronger than that, when you think of what it takes to have a baby. It's a really big deal, having a commit-ment to a person for the rest of its life. If you're forcing some-body to have a baby, making a lifetime decision against their will, then problems are going to turn up and they're not going to be very happy about that. They're probably going to be ex-tremely depressed.

I feel abortion is a part of life. Having a child or not having a child is a basic fundamental right for men and women. The size of one's family is a basic fundamental right. I could just as easily work in a fertility clinic as an abortion clinic, or in an adoption agency, because it is all part of the rich texture of people's lives. That they are able to choose what they want to do. I don't see it as any different. Women come in here who have a newborn baby and are breastfeeding, and with small children. So many different types of women. Handicapped women. Very, very young women. Old women who thought they were past menopause. Very working-class women, very rich women. So the world goes by here.

Good Reasons for Abortions

An unappreciated but primary reason women have abortions is that contraception so often fails. If you don't think so, con-sider this: under the caption "Sins of Emission," a 1990 *London Guardian* squib informs us that Canadian researchers found that condoms leak during intercourse nearly three times out of four. Three times out of four!

What are we supposed to do when our birth control method fails? When the cap fails, the pill fails, the condom fails? The fact is that contraceptive failure led to 1.6 to 2 million of the 3.3 million unwanted pregnancies in the United States in 1987.

"Such pregnancies constitute about half of the 1.5 million abortions performed each year." This is not the conclusion of some fly-by-night quack institute or radical political group. This is the finding of the National Academy of Sciences in 1990.

Washingtoon © M.A. Stamaty. Reprinted by permission.

Now, against this very good reason for an abortion—leaky condoms and faulty IUDs—what reasons do women give researchers? Here are the latest findings. A 1987 survey of 1,900 women at 30 abortion facilities asked, "Why do women have abortions?" The women could give as many reasons as they wanted, and most women do not have just one reason, but a complex of motives. Here are the top six reasons all women gave, the percentages being those for women under 18:

1. Concerned about how having a baby could change her life, 92 percent
2. Not mature enough or too young to have a child, 81 percent
3. Can't afford baby now, 73 percent
4. Doesn't want others to know she has had sex or is pregnant, 42 percent
5. Has relationship problems and doesn't want to be a single parent, 37 percent
6. Unready for the responsibility, 33 percent

There have been many studies done with smaller groups that expressed exactly the same reasons. Older women are more likely to say their families are complete; younger women more likely to say a baby would interfere with their education, career, and personal freedom. At any age, women say they have too many responsibilities already and not enough money.

The American Public Does Not Approve

The reasons for which the American public at large is most approving of abortion are not the foremost reasons why women have abortions. Women, in the main, do not have abortions because of rape, incest, deformed fetuses, or because their physical life is in danger. But these are the most appropriate reasons in the eyes of the American public. Being poor, too young, unmarried, and not wanting a baby are deemed less valid in public opinion polls. We have a huge disjunction here that needs to be resolved. And the pathetic thing, in terms of public opinion, is that "I don't want a baby at the moment" isn't considered the most valid reason at all.

Women have abortions because their contraception failed and because they did not want to have a baby at that time. But anyone who thinks women take those two realities lightly hasn't spent a day observing abortion providers.

> It is a major life occasion. Especially seeing all these different women, it can be one of the most profound decisions that you make. Because, yes, it is a very safe medical procedure, but there are risks, just as there are to all medical procedures, and you could be one of those very few statistics. It is a life decision because if you carry to term, your entire life is going to change forever. And by choosing not to, you are also making a choice to lead your life in one particular direction. A lot of women say things like, I know this is right for me because I'm in school, I don't have any money, I want to be a lawyer and I haven't even finished high school yet. And I know I want to do these things, and to have a child right now would mean I could never do these things. A lot of people say that. It definitely makes people think and want to change, or reinforces their decision and their life choices. (*24-year-old abortion counselor*)

Another fact related to reasons for abortion is that the majority of abortions are first abortions. Among Canadian women, 78 percent of women having abortions had no prior abortion, and among women in England and Wales, the figure is 82 percent. For 60 percent of American women who have abortions, it is their first.

Still a Valid Reason

If it is a second, third, or fourth abortion, the reason "I don't want a baby at the moment" is no less valid. If you are not comfortable with the idea of multiple abortions, the old adage of walking in someone else's shoes comes to mind.

Sometimes people who have three or four or five abortions are failing in every other area of their lives in terms of being victimized. And they're taking such responsibility in making those decisions—where they don't feel they have control in any other area—to have an abortion. When they clearly know they aren't capable of being a good parent, or being a parent again. I give these women a lot of credit. Sometimes people get down on women who have repeat abortions without looking at those women's lives. They aren't willing to look at each pregnancy as a separate event with its own set of circumstances. And it doesn't matter how many times a woman has had an abortion, it only matters in her own eyes and her own value system. The last thing women who are having more than one abortion need is to feel judged and put down and criticized. They're doing the best they can, and in some cases are doing a great job of making decisions when they don't feel much control in other parts of their lives. (*47-year-old social worker, abortion at 22*) . . .

Deciding About Children

For people asking if they can be a parent now, Marjory Skowronski has written an abortion decision-making book, *Abortion and Alternatives*, that contains two lists of questions concerning our feelings about children. Her questions are good at any time—before an abortion, after an abortion, and at times when abortion isn't an issue.

Here is my paraphrasing of Skowronski's lists (p. 46, pp. 98–99) about children. Anyone thinking about parenting should at the very least write a short essay about each.

1. How well do I relate to children? How much do I enjoy children?
2. Do I want to have a child now? Ever? What do I think is the ideal age and time for me to have a child? Why?
3. If yes to a child, why? What are my motivations for wanting to have children? (Can you think of five? Which is number one?)
4. Do I feel any pressure from other people to have children? Who? Why do they feel that way?
5. How much time do I want to spend in child rearing? On a day-to-day basis? In terms of years (each child taking at least 18 years)?
6. Do I resent unforeseen interruptions in my daily schedule? How do I picture myself working and raising a child at the same time?
7. As far as work goes, am I finished with my schooling and professional training? What are my future school and training plans? What job is my goal?
8. How do women who do that job raise children at the same time?

9. Am I financially independent? If not, when will I be? What kind of job will I have and how much money will I need to be making to consider myself financially independent?
10. How does a child fit in with the kind of life I want to live?
11. What can I offer a child in terms of my capacities as a parent?

The Best Reason

Not wanting a child strongly is the best possible reason to have an abortion. Prochoice women *with* children say it most convincingly. A 27-year-old accountant had two abortions, at 17 and 20. The second abortion prompted her to plan her life completely from that point on.

> When you're pregnant and you don't want to be, it's an intense crisis. For me it brought out my true feelings about having kids, and during that time I realized, Yes, I do want to have kids. And that turned out to be a true idea. I have a baby now and it's very wonderful. I am more strongly prochoice now, having had a child. It is such a wonderful experience that no one should go through that unless they want that. And kids are so wonderful that you should only have one if you want one. So an abortion is just as big a decision as deciding to have a child. How can it be fundamentally wrong to try to raise children in the best way you know how? And sometimes that means doing things that seem really contradictory. In the end you have to do what you think is going to be the best for your family, for yourself, for your future children. Now that I'm a parent I'm making those decisions every day. What's going to be the best? For our family, for my son. And these decisions are not a comfortable thing. There's a tremendous amount of guilt involved in parenting. You have to make the decision that you think is going to be best. And ultimately you only have to defend it to yourself.

The abortion decision is complex and complicated for many women. It may mean we have to relinquish our fantasies and face reality from now on. It may mean being the most responsible we'll ever be in our whole life, *right now*. It can bring us face to face with our stated goals and whether we're seriously striving to attain them. It brings out women's strengths to decide about abortion. . . .

Making the Decision

The National Abortion Federation's (NAF) "guide to making the right decision for you" poses these questions for the decision-making process:

> "What are two or three things that matter most to me in my life right now?"

> "What are two or three things that I hope to have or achieve in the next five or ten years?"

"What would I lose or give up in the next five or ten years if I have the baby? Place the baby for adoption? Have an abortion?"

"How would other people react who matter to me if I have the baby? Place the baby for adoption? Have an abortion?"

These questions concern the three basic choices we face when we are pregnant. But every decision involves a small set of basic choices. Every decision affects what we hope to achieve in the next five or ten years. Every choice we make means we gain something *and* lose something. And every decision touches our partners, parents, and friends.

"Although a new child would disrupt her work . . . that did not seem cause enough [to have an abortion]."

An Unwanted Pregnancy Does Not Justify an Abortion

Faith Abbott

In the following viewpoint, Faith Abbott discusses the choices made by two women—each in their thirties with three children already—who unexpectedly became pregnant. According to Abbott, both women were initially dismayed by the news; one chose to end the pregnancy with an abortion, while the other, after some misgivings, decided to keep her baby. The mother who decided to keep her baby found her daughter to be a continual source of joy and delight, Abbott contends, a joy never to be known by the woman who aborted her baby. Abbott is a contributing editor to *Human Life Review*.

As you read, consider the following questions:

1. Why did Elizabeth Klein and her husband decide against an abortion, according to Abbott?
2. What reasons does Elinor Nelson give for her decision to have an abortion, as cited by the author?
3. In what ways is Elizabeth Klein's "bonus baby" different from her three other children, according to Abbott?

Faith Abbott, "A Tale of Two Women," *Human Life Review*, Spring 1993. Reprinted with permission.

"When I found I was pregnant, I had not been pleased."

—Elizabeth Klein, in *Hers* column, *New York Times Magazine*,
August 27, 1989

"When she told me the test was positive, I felt shock begin to set in."

—Elinor Nelson, *First Person* section, *San Francisco Chronicle*,
June 9, 1992

As I was weeding my files—Spring Gleaning—I found these two articles I'd saved. As I read them again, I was fascinated by what two mothers of three had in common and by how different were their "choices" about the fourth child.

An Older Mother

Elizabeth Klein, a writer and poet, begins the "Hers" feature with "They had labeled me 'Older Mother.'" The "They" were doctors at an antenatal clinic in England, where she and her husband were spending a year; she was in the hospital because she had developed a bladder infection in the eighth month of pregnancy, and the doctors wanted to keep her off her feet while the infection cleared up. Her third child was nine years old, and she had been looking forward to more freedom to finish her novel; the unplanned fourth baby ("a failure of birth control") would, if she had it, arrive in time for Klein's 40th birthday.

Friends had asked: "What about your writing? You have three lovely children. You've done your part." Indeed, Klein writes, "influenced by the zero population growth movement, certain acquaintances suggested we had done too much." She herself had signed petitions "and fought for every woman's right to have an abortion" but, she writes, "in this case, at least, I didn't think it was for me. At best, abortion is a difficult, painful choice—not something to be done without great need." She was married to a man she loved, a good father. They weren't starving, and their children—well on the way to adolescence—were delighted with the idea of a baby. Although a new child would disrupt her work and the "liberation from child care" she and her husband had been looking forward to, that did not seem cause enough. "An abortion, we both felt, would throw into question the way we saw the treasured family we already had."

Unfortunately, she says, her maternal instincts did not respond to reason: when a young friend placed her baby in her arms, she found herself looking with distaste into "a little scrunched face inspiring no tenderness, only intense tedium at the thought of tending him. What was I going to do with a baby I couldn't return to his mother?" She arranged to have amniocentesis once they got to England, though she was not sure—despite her reservations—what it would cost her emotionally to have an abortion if something were wrong. When told she had as much chance of having a miscarriage from the amniocentesis as she did, at her age, of having a Down syndrome child, she hoped for the miscarriage: "That is until, lying on the table where the procedure was to take place, I saw the ultrasound scan on a television monitor above me reveal the perfectly shaped head of the child I carried. I wanted that baby!"

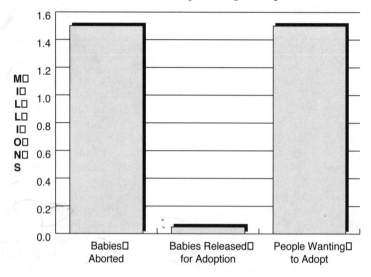

Annual Abortions and New Adoptable Babies

Plus those currently wanting to adopt

Source: Randy Alcorn, *ProLife Answers to ProChoice Arguments*, 1992.

In the years since, she writes, "I have been enormously grateful that the possibility of abortion changed my late pregnancy from an accident to a choice. Once our little girl was born, we could not imagine our world without her, a joy undiminished by the wearying reflection that, when she leaves for college, my husband and I will have been parenting for 31 years."

Shocking News

The title of Elizabeth Klein's piece is "Bonus Baby." The second woman's article is titled "Infertility, Triplets—And an Abortion." When Elinor Nelson was told her pregnancy test was positive, the shock set in; she paused "for what felt like an eternity" and then asked "What do I do now?" The doctor's answer was: "That depends on whether you want it." Achieving a pregnancy through normal means was a miracle, but through in vitro fertilization she'd had triplet boys, then two years old and creating havoc in the next room. The prospect of another baby in eight months was, "to say the least, daunting."

She phoned her husband (he's there in the picture above the article, with her and their three sons: the caption says "After years of struggling with infertility, Nelson, to her dismay, conceived naturally") and shared "the shocking news." They agreed that they didn't want another baby "and this generated enormous guilt" but they were in no condition to make any decisions, and got off the phone "each with this monumental piece of news entering our own twilight zone." Thus began what Nelson calls the two longest and most difficult weeks of her life. The only positive thing that emerged from this "short-lived hell" was the odd feeling that her unwanted pregnancy made her feel almost like an average woman—it was, after all, the most normal of her reproductive experiences: "Conceiving three babies in a laboratory dish, after weeks of hormone injections, blood tests, ultrasounds and a doctor's game of darts with my ovaries, was hardly mainstream. But an unplanned pregnancy? This was downright pedestrian."

The morning after Nelson had got "the shocking news" about her pregnancy, she and her husband awoke to a scene of almost mass destruction in their boys' room. One boy had scaled the side of the bureau and had pulled down lamp, cassette recorder, and all the books from a high shelf. Mother and father looked at each other, having the same thought: "Imagine awakening to this mayhem with the added attraction of a screaming baby in the next room. We must be out of our minds to contemplate having another baby." Although the fact that she had gotten pregnant was simply amazing, she writes, the prospect of another baby in their home was overwhelming. Husband and wife outlined all the reasons for "terminating the pregnancy"; the "bottom line" was that they were managing their sons well, most of the time, but "we simply didn't see how we could fit another child into our busy lives."

Making the Decision

She worried that this baby, even if healthy, might be "the piece of the puzzle that pushed us over the edge to become a dysfunctional family." And what if the baby had a serious medical problem? Adoption was not an option, she writes: "If I was going to carry a baby, I would keep it. I knew what it was like to go through a pregnancy, to feel the unborn child. If I went through that, it would be mine. . . . But the thought of lying on that table and having that life sucked out of me was repellent." Her "usually logical mind" was not functioning; it felt like mush: she couldn't even begin a decision-making process. The best advice she received was from an old friend and former abortion counselor, Lori, who suggested she try to determine how the prospect of another baby made her "feel." Nelson realized that although she did have some loving feelings, she mostly felt stress and anxiety, and the prospect of trying to juggle another child into her household left her panicky. Lori's greatest contribution was to provide Nelson "with permission":

> Simply because I was 34, happily married, financially comfortable, with a nice home, loving my children and surviving a history of infertility did not disqualify me from having an abortion. Furthermore, that all of my previous reproductive choices had been taken away did not mean that this one had to be eliminated as well. I decided to have the abortion.

The editors gave that section its own subtitle: "Choices Remain." A few days later, though, she and her husband found out why anti-abortion activists "like to display pictures of fetuses." When she underwent the ultrasound to rule out a tubal pregnancy (made likely by the anatomical problems that had caused the infertility) she hadn't told the radiologist about the planned abortion, and he pointed out not just the location of the fetus but also its heartbeat and measurements, and "We dragged ourselves out of the office feeling horrible." That night her husband confessed to second thoughts, but said he still felt the ultimate decision was hers. "The ultrasound," she writes, "made me feel the loss more keenly, but I still did not want the baby." Three days later they arrived at the abortion clinic—thankful that it was off the beaten path, away from any protesters, and that the staff was friendly and understanding. The waiting room was "filled with a true cross-section of the community. No one looked happy. No one was chatting with anyone but their partners. This was not a day to make friends." The abortion itself was uncomfortable, though she had gone through many infertility procedures that were much worse.

> I tried to concentrate on the physical feelings, not on what was happening. It was over in minutes, and I was overcome with sadness. "I'm so sorry I didn't want you," I told the fetus. "I'm so sorry."

For several days she felt a depression stronger than the ones she'd had during the years of hormone-altering fertility drugs. She says she didn't regret having the abortion, but she felt terrible about not wanting that baby. The fog finally lifted; "feelings of sadness have recurred, but never that mind-altering depression" and "Now we look at our three bright, beautiful and very energetic sons, and we are thrilled with our family. Seeing other people's babies has not changed our minds. We are secure in our decision." Having the abortion, she says, was a dreadful experience; the best thing she can say about it is that it is over. And that she had it.

Two Choices

So these are the two stories: Elizabeth Klein, having a fourth child at age 40—old enough to be the mother of her hospital ward-mates—knowing that a new baby would disrupt her work, but wanting that baby, and deciding that an abortion would throw into question the way they saw the treasured family they already had; Elinor Nelson, a younger woman who didn't see how she and her husband could fit another baby "into their busy lives" and who didn't want the baby, anyway, and feared that if she had it they might become a dysfunctional family. Elizabeth Klein cannot imagine her world without her "bonus baby" daughter, who was 10 when the article was published. Klein remembers that on a tour of prospective colleges with their oldest daughter, the youngest had just been toilet-trained and they found "as much need to investigate the public facilities as the library holdings." When the last of the older children went off to school, she and her husband couldn't spontaneously join their friends for dinner or the movies: it was back to baby-sitting. So there were inconveniences, and sometimes embarrassments—such as when the little one's friends would think her father was her grandfather. But Klein writes that "Having one child depending on us for entertainment and information has made us aware of how much our older children amused and taught each other." And "We have found special pleasure in having our 'bonus baby' now that her siblings are away. We have the kind of close conversation with her at dinner that was rarely possible when our noisy three-some was at the table." (You wonder how Elinor Nelson would feel, if she read that.) Bonus Baby and her mother "enjoy an easy intimacy, her questions about the adult world recalling those I asked in my own girlhood as an only child. She loves to report the responses over the telephone to her brothers and sister for verification, and delights, as I do, in the abundant love she receives from them even at a distance."

A Rich and Satisfying Relationship

Elizabeth Klein travels a lot, leading workshops and giving readings; she feels guilty for leaving her daughter so much but is regularly and endearingly reprieved by the sight of the colorful "Welcome Home Mom!" banners taped on the mantel. "Older mother and young daughter, our relationship is rich—unsettling and satisfying, as is any relationship bound by love." Elinor Nelson might have come to enjoy her Bonus Baby too, but she refused the gift.

"Life is difficult enough as it is. It didn't make sense to us to start [a baby] out with a severe problem, to go into it knowing."

Congenital Defects May Justify Abortion

Kate Maloy and Maggie Jones Patterson

In the following viewpoint, a married couple who were interviewed by Kate Maloy and Maggie Jones Patterson tell of their decision to abort their five-month-old fetus after discovering that the baby would be born with Down's syndrome. The couple contends that the energy and time it would take to raise a handicapped child would have adversely affected their careers and their relationship with their daughter. Although the couple felt guilty and sad about the abortion, they believe they made the right decision. Maloy and Patterson are the authors of *Birth or Abortion? Private Struggles in a Political World*, from which this viewpoint is taken.

As you read, consider the following questions:

1. What made Natalie and Richard change their minds about amniocentesis, according to the authors?
2. What reason do Natalie and Richard give for choosing to abort a fetus with Down's syndrome when they would have carried to term a fetus with hydrocephalus?
3. What did Natalie say was a contributing factor in her decision to get pregnant again after her abortion?

Natalie Murdoch and her husband, Richard Meyer, planned carefully so that the birth of their second child would coincide roughly with their daughter Amanda's third birthday. . . .

Natalie was thirty-four when she conceived, and she would have been thirty-five at delivery. This meant the risk of Down syndrome had just drawn even with the risk of a miscarriage caused by amniocentesis. Natalie was not sure whether she wanted to undergo the test.

Natalie and Richard planned carefully for everything in their lives. All the furnishings in their remodeled home on the eastern edge of Cleveland have been carefully selected for function and aesthetics. The couple thought and talked about major decisions, closely examining their reactions and anticipating the effects of change before acting. . . .

"We spent a lot of dinner time just talking about amnio for almost four months," Natalie said. She and Richard went to genetic counseling, and, with no history of genetic problems on either side of their family, finally decided to forego amniocentesis unless an alphafetoprotein (AFP) test indicated a higher-than-average risk of Down syndrome. AFP levels in maternal blood serum can, in addition to indicating neural tube defects, refine the statistical chances that a child will have Down syndrome. Unless Natalie's AFP test increased her age-related odds, which were one in 350, she intended to refuse further prenatal testing.

Fear of a Late-Term Abortion

"Part of the debate that we had for four months was that I really was terrified about having a needle stuck into my 4½-month pregnant stomach," Natalie said. Another factor in her aversion to the test was the idea of choosing abortion in her second trimester if the results of the amniocentesis were bad. Although she had already had a very early abortion when she was in college and was still very pro-choice politically, Natalie said: "I knew that I would feel very differently about it this time around. I had some moral reservations about a late abortion. With the first abortion I had never had a full-term pregnancy. But now I knew what a baby was like at 4½ months. I had been through it, I had read all the books."

Natalie's AFP level slightly *reduced* her risk of having a baby with Down syndrome, from one in 350 to one in 367, and she informed her doctor that she had decided against amniocentesis. When the doctor very gently asked why, Natalie explained her fear of the needle used in amniocentesis and her uneasiness about terminating a pregnancy in the fifth month. "And then," Natalie said, "she posed the question in a way that I don't think Richard and I ever did in all the months we debated it. She said: 'Would it be more difficult for you to terminate the pregnancy at this point or to raise a child with Down syndrome for the rest of your life?' And I just started to cry 'cause I knew what the answer to the question was, but I wished I didn't feel the way that I did."

When Natalie decided to proceed with amniocentesis after all, Richard was relieved. "I had always felt that the amnio was the right thing to do," he said, "and had never quite felt like I could come out and actually say that, because a lot of Natalie's fear was about the procedure itself. That was something she had to go through and not me. So it was easy for me to sit back and talk about the risks and benefits when I was the person who wasn't taking any of the risk and didn't have to face getting stuck with a needle."

Natalie was in her seventeenth week when she went into the hospital for the procedure she had feared so much. That part, she told us, "was a piece of cake." But Natalie was not to emerge from the test without confronting a worse fear—one that was revealed in her ultrasound test. The first sign of a problem was the intensity with which the physician conducting the ultrasound test peered repeatedly into the screen. With him was an entourage of other medical personnel, staring with him.

The Odds Increase

"I didn't think much of it," Natalie recalled, "because it's a teaching hospital, and they always have entourages of people. But they just kept pressing on my stomach and redoing the sonar." Finally, her doctor whispered to her that the baby's head looked too large. When Richard questioned the doctors further, they told him there was about a 20 percent chance that the measurement reflected hydrocephalus, a condition characterized by excess fluid in the cranium. Yet, there was an 80 percent chance that it was merely within the range of error for the sonar equipment. That seemed reassuring, but the odds that something was wrong with the baby had suddenly gone from one in 367 to one in five. The doctors wanted to redo the cranial measurement in three weeks. The amniocentesis results were expected in four weeks.

During those three weeks before the next ultrasound test, Natalie and Richard, who works for the county health department, searched the literature for information about hydrocephalus. They learned that it could range from a treatable condition to one that would prove fatal soon after birth. They decided, said Richard, that, "if there was any real chance that surgery could correct the baby's problem, we would go ahead and not terminate the pregnancy."

The next day, as Natalie was feeding Amanda a late Sunday breakfast, her doctor called. The amniocentesis results had come back early. Natalie and Richard's baby had Down syndrome. Natalie, telling this part of her story, began to cry. Richard, too, had been stunned. After all their research on hydrocephalus, he had almost forgotten about the amniocentesis test. Ironically, there was no relationship between the seemingly abnormal ultrasound reading and the diagnosis of Down syndrome.

Starting Out with Joy Instead of Grief

Phyllis and Joel Blume came together to Phyllis's first appointment with me. That in itself was a little unusual—I don't often meet the husbands of my gynecological patients at our first encounter unless there's a specific reason, like a baby on the way. . . .

"We've always wanted children," Phyllis began. "Several. But I think you should know, our parents are from Eastern Europe, on both sides. So before we got married, we were tested for Tay-Sachs disease. I'm a carrier, and so is Joel.". . .

Tay-Sachs is a death sentence. There is no cure, no treatment. Newborns who have it appear normal, but within a few months they begin to deteriorate, losing muscle tone and brain function until they die, usually by the age of three. I wanted to be sure the Blumes knew what could happen. They did. . . .

Phyllis became pregnant, right on schedule. She and Joel started out saying that they would take their chances, and if the baby was born with Tay-Sachs, they would love it just the same. But as the pregnancy became a reality to them, they began to understand that the trauma of bearing a child only to watch it die would be devastating to their lives and their hopes for a family. . . .

I had to tell Phyllis that the news was bad. She and Joel chose termination.

Less than a year later, she was pregnant again. This time, the news was good. In due course, I was able to hand Joel and Phyllis a normal, healthy son. "We did the right thing," Joel said. "I wasn't sure, you know. But to have started out in grief instead of this—that would have been wrong. What joy!"

Today the couple has three healthy, growing children.

Don Sloan, *Abortion: A Doctor's Perspective/A Woman's Dilemma*, 1992.

Natalie and Richard knew immediately that they would terminate the pregnancy. To some, their decision to abort a baby with Down syndrome might seem inconsistent with their willingness to keep one with hydrocephalus. Natalie tried to explain their thinking: "We knew if the child had Down, the child had Down.

Yes, there were varying degrees of Down and varying abnormalities that were associated with it, but there was no hope that this child was ever going to have anything but Down. There was no way of curing it or lessening it, which we understood there to be with hydrocephalus."

Natalie's doctor repeatedly invited questions and asked Natalie if she and Richard were sure about their decision, but Natalie assured her that she and Richard were unwavering. . . . "I know all of the things about how a seriously handicapped child brings a lot to your life that you wouldn't get otherwise," Natalie said. "A seriously handicapped child takes a lot from your life that you wouldn't otherwise have to give," she added. "I think life is difficult enough as it is. It didn't make sense to us to start [a baby] out with a severe problem, to go into it knowing."

Other Time Commitments

Along with their unwillingness to burden a child with a handicap whose severity could not be known ahead of time, Richard and Natalie were also afraid that raising such a child might deprive Amanda of necessary time and attention. Richard explained, "I guess we knew that a Down child would require, at best, constant care from us, and that would take a great deal away from Amanda."

Their careers were another consideration. "Both of us are in jobs that are a lot more than jobs. They're things that we do because we believe in the work," said Richard, who works in public health. Natalie is an architect. Both jobs require commitments of time and emotion, which they willingly give. "All those things would have been affected by a life of caring for a Down child," Richard said. Natalie thought she would probably have to quit her job—one of the things a handicapped child could take from her life.

Natalie entered the hospital for an abortion two days after she took the devastating call from her doctor. Doctors injected the amniotic sac surrounding the fetus with a saline solution. Then, Richard and Natalie waited nearly twenty-four hours for the contractions that would allow her to expel the dead fetus and placenta. Their sorrow was compounded by anger at the nurses, who seemed unsympathetic. Finally, at 6:30 in the evening, the day after the saline injection, and after hours of contractions, Natalie felt a sudden release of pressure. The nurse told her her water had broken, and she took the bedpan to empty it. "Richard turned to me," Natalie recalled, "and said, 'I think you just had the baby.' And I said, 'Well, it sure felt like more than just water to me.'" Richard left to corner the nurses, who confirmed that Natalie had delivered the fetus. By then, Natalie was too physically and emotionally drained to become angry.

Richard asked to see the baby. He had been caught up in Natalie's trauma and had been unable to indulge his own feelings until then. Alone in an empty room with his dead baby boy, Richard wept. He was still overcome when he returned to Natalie's room. "It was stunning to me because I've known him for a long time and I've never seen him cry," Natalie said.

Natalie herself had thought she would not want to see the baby, but she changed her mind. She had worried about the possibility of a mix-up in lab results, and seeing the baby put her worries to rest. "As tiny as he was, it was very clear that he had Down. I mean he was very tiny, but he had deeply webbed fingers and his ears were set very far back and his eyes were wide apart. . . . I mean, there was no question that that baby really did have Down."

Guilty Feelings

When she returned home from the hospital, Natalie wanted to cut herself off from the world. "I just wanted to go in a dark cave and not have to deal with anything at all," Natalie said. She felt guilty. A social worker who had counseled her in the hospital suggested that Natalie participate in a pregnancy loss group. Natalie followed that advice for a while, but she could not identify with the other women, who felt guilty after losing babies through miscarriage or stillbirth. No one else had gone through an abortion. Natalie said: "I just wanted to scream: 'You don't know anything about guilt. You didn't do anything.'"

Richard felt very little guilt. "What I did feel, often, was angry that nobody really understood what had happened to us," Richard said. "Not angry at them, but angry at the way society treats this sort of thing. You know, I think that the world seems to be about evenly divided into two camps. One camp is the people who think that any kind of abortion, including the kind we had for genetic reasons, is a sin and probably ought to be a crime, and the other camp thinks it's sort of a convenient medical procedure. But nobody really responded to it like a great personal tragedy for Natalie and me. That's not part of the public debate."

Richard admitted the physical reality of being pregnant made the emotional impact more intense for Natalie. "I felt that baby kicking," she said, and it took her much longer to recover. During the year that followed the abortion, Natalie continued to grieve and feel guilty as she passed a number of anniversaries: the baby's due date, the dates of the bad news, and the date of the abortion. When we spoke to her, she was pregnant again. "Our chances are much higher now that we've had a Down fetus," Natalie said. "For some reason they don't understand, once you have a Down baby, the recurrence rate goes to one in a hundred—bingo—for all ages."

Natalie asserted that her and her husband's decision to abort their Down syndrome fetus was the right one and that they would do the same thing again. But her conviction was weakened somewhat by the fact that she had decided to proceed differently this time, opting for CVS instead of amniocentesis. The test is done as early as the eighth week and delivers results in days, thus allowing a first-trimester abortion if chromosomal abnormalities are diagnosed. "My best guess," Natalie said, "is that if the CVS were not available . . . I don't think I would have tried to get pregnant again." Natalie said she was not, in fact, prepared to repeat a second-trimester abortion. "You're starting to get to the point where the fetus could live, possibly, outside the womb," she pointed out. She said she would still abort her current pregnancy if she had to, but she would not have felt the baby kicking or heard its heartbeat. "While I think that what we did was right, it was emotionally more difficult because the baby was becoming more human as it got older," she said.

A few weeks after our interview, Natalie's CVS revealed that she was carrying a girl in normal health. She was relieved but still not able to put all the pain and guilt of her abortion behind her. It was not until that baby was born six months later that Natalie seemed at peace—with herself and with the newborn daughter who would not exist except for the loss of the tiny fetal boy with Down syndrome.

Richard encapsulated their experience, saying thoughtfully: "I think if it had been some years earlier, when amniocentesis wasn't available, and we had had a Down child come to term . . . we would have done our best to raise the child and give it all the love we could. I think we could have done a good job of raising a Down child. But we had the choice. One of the good things and one of the terrifying things about technology is it gives you that kind of choice."

> *"How wrong it is to think of Down's children as something 'other,' a mere aberration of nature."*

Congenital Defects Do Not Justify Abortion

Dominic Lawson

Dominic Lawson, an editor of the London *Sunday Telegraph*, is the father of a daughter with Down's syndrome. In the following viewpoint, he maintains that aborting a fetus because of a deformity is reprehensible and is a form of eugenics. Lawson argues that a baby born with a mental or physical handicap will not necessarily be an unhappy person. All children have a right to life, he contends, whether or not they are handicapped.

As you read, consider the following questions:

1. What was Lawson's reaction to the consultant's diagnosis of his daughter's Down's syndrome?
2. Why is it increasingly improbable that children with Down's syndrome will be born, in Lawson's opinion?
3. Why did Lawson and his wife decide not to "have the tests" for Down's syndrome?

Dominic Lawson, "All You Need Is Life," *Spectator*, June 17, 1995. Reprinted with permission.

After only two and a half hours' labour Domenica emerged at lunchtime on Thursday 1 June 1995, with a shocked, empty stare on her face. She was also completely blue and inert. 'Slow coming round' was the midwife's later, written, observation. Only when the six-pound five-ounce form was finally bullied into breathing did I finally stop asking—in the useless way in which fathers drive busy midwives demented—'Will she be all right? Will she be all right?'

The Diagnosis

But even after my own abject panic was ended by hearing the first splutterings of a pair of tiny lungs, there remained in the room a faint but palpable tension. The duty pediatrician did not smile while she examined Domenica with what looked, even to my untrained eyes, like professional concern. Then she wheeled the little baby out of the room, and asked me to follow both of them down the corridor, to the office of the senior consultant.

He went through a similar rigmarole of clinical examination, all the while asking a series of seemingly irrelevant questions: what was the condition of any other of my children? what sort of pregnancy had this been? Perfectly normal, I said, except that my wife had broken her leg in four places, half way through her confinement, and was still on crutches. The consultant seemed not to hear this last remark, and interrupted my off-pat explanation of how Rosa had sustained a quadruple spiral fracture of her right leg while trying to get into her car.

'Yes, well, we have a problem.'

'What?'

'I am certain that your daughter has Down's syndrome.'

This came as an enormous relief. Since our second daughter, Natalia, had emerged too premature even for the magic of modern medicine, at 22 weeks' gestation, I had been morbidly anxious throughout the succeeding pregnancy. The consultant's 'We have a problem' I instantly interpreted as 'This one won't make it, either'. His 'Your daughter has Down's syndrome' sounded more to me like 'But this one will live'.

The doctor then repeated his earlier clinical examination, this time giving me an idiot's guide to my daughter's ten-minute-old body. 'Here, you see her grip is very weak. She is very floppy. Her head has three fontanelles, instead of the normal two. And, here, her tongue is very large. If you look at her eyes, you'll notice these epicanthal folds, and a slightly Asiatic appearance. If you look at her ears, you might be able to see how they are folded over at the helix. You notice, here, that there are some extra folds of skin behind her neck. Now, if you look at her feet, here, and here, you'll see that there is an unusually large gap between the big and and first toes. These, I'm afraid, are all phenotypes of Down's syndrome. Now, to be absolutely certain, we can take a blood sample, and do a chromosomal analysis. But that would be a formality in this case, and is not necessary for my diagnosis.'

Anger, Love, and Grief

Two emotions coursed through me as the consultant gave me a guided tour of the stigmata of Down's syndrome. The first was anger. While I understood that the doctor was only doing his professional duty—to explain as clearly and as quickly as possible the condition of his patient—I wanted to shout out, 'This is my daughter you are prodding, not some random strip of flesh.' The second emotion was love.

This surprised me. While I love my eldest daughter, Savannah, it took me many months to do so. During the earliest part of her life I found her endlessly fascinating, and a source of great pride, but I did not feel the pang of love. I gather that this is quite common among new fathers. Or, at least, that is what I told my wife. Yet now, after so little and so strange an introduction, I felt an intense, almost physically painful love for this third daughter.

Happy and Productive Lives

Down's syndrome children are becoming extinct. Most are now aborted before they can be born.

Ninety percent of Down's children are only mildly to moderately retarded. And while they are prone to a wide variety of physical ailments, nearly all are treatable. In fact, most Down's children, with love and care, can live happy, productive, surprisingly independent lives.

Francis X. Maier, *Commonweal*, March 26, 1993.

It would be a sin of omission not to record that in the succeeding days I did not also feel a sense of grief. Grief at the thought that Domenica's life expectancy is not much more than half her elder sister's. Grief at the thought that she will almost certainly not experience the joy of having children herself. But this grief always coexisted with the feeling of elation which accompanies birth. It is a dizzying mix of emotions, this combination of sadness and elation, and I suspect it is appreciation of this that lies behind the anxiety with which some friends approach us. They want to sympathise and they want to congratulate, but how do they do both at the same time?

My wife has experienced a different form of grief, which, say all the textbooks, is absolutely characteristic of mothers in this predicament. They grieve for the loss of the child they thought they were carrying. Many mothers-to-be seem to have a very clear idea of the nature of the person who is squirming and kicking in their belly. That person does not have Down's syndrome, with all the attendant problems, both physical and mental. But this sense of two different people, the imaginary perfect child and the real handicapped one, is, of course, no more than a powerful illusion.

Genetic in Origin

It is not even as though Down's syndrome is something which afflicts normal children in the womb, as a result of stress or illness, although that was what many doctors tended to believe until 1959, when a French professor named Jérôme Lejeune declared that the characteristic features of Down's syndrome were genetic in origin. He discovered that the Down's children had 47 chromosomes in every DNA molecule, instead of the normal 46, and that this extra genetic material, amounting to no more than about 50 to 100 genes in all, was the cause of all the differences which later come to light—the sort of differences which my daughter's pediatrician was so anxious to explain to me.

The DNA make-up of a person is settled almost at the moment of conception, when the female and male nuclei, which contain the chromosomes that will endow the offspring with his or her hereditary characteristics, fuse to form a single nucleus. The extra characteristics of the future Down's baby are caused during the first cellular subdivision of that nucleus, when 47 chromosomes are created rather than 46. This cellular self-multiplication is then repeated constantly for approximately 266 days, at the end of which you have a baby ready for delivery.

It is worth spelling this process out because it demonstrates first, that the Down's baby is as much a product of his or her parents' genes (and of their parents') as any other child, and second, that there is no sense in which the Down's baby could ever have been constructed in any other way, once conception had occurred. There is no possible alternative Domenica Lawson without Down's syndrome. That is her identity, her very essence, along with all the other genes she has inherited from us.

Her elder sister was formed by a different merging of the same parental genes, along more orthodox lines. . . . And the extraordinary similarities of these two girls, at least as babies, also illustrates how wrong it is to think of Down's children as something 'other', a mere aberration of nature. Despite all the peculiarities outlined by Domenica's pediatrician, she looks like a twin of her sister, as I am constantly reminded by the picture of

Savannah aged two weeks which I carry in my wallet. They have a number of identical facial expressions. And, exactly as Savannah did, Domenica sleeps in an absurd parody of deep thought, with her right fore-finger resting on her top lip and her right thumb appearing to prop up her chin.

One visitor, a good friend who has the endearing habit of uttering exactly what is on her mind, exclaimed with relief upon seeing Domenica, 'Oh, I was so frightened about what she would look like. But she looks just like her sister.' I do not repeat all this out of parental pride—or not just out of parental pride—but to make the point, again, that the Down's children are not monsters formed at random. Of course Domenica's intellectual and physical progress will never be as rapid or fluent as her sister's, and it will doubtless cost both her and us enormous amounts of effort. But the point is, she will continue to develop, however slowly, along lines which will reveal her to be a true mixture of the genes which her parents married in order to perpetuate.

The Risks Involved

And yet. And yet a whole industry has been developed to make it increasingly improbable that children like Domenica Lawson will be allowed to live. In England, the National Health Service advises all mothers-to-be over 35 to undergo medical procedures which extract fluid from around the foetus, which is then subjected to chromosomal analysis. The NHS provides this service free because the probability of Down's syndrome—far and away the commonest form of congenital mental handicap in the population—appears to grow rapidly when the mother's age increases beyond the mid-thirties.

But these procedures, either chorionic villus sampling or amniosentisis, have a significantly higher statistical risk of causing miscarriage than the 36-year-old mother has of carrying a Down's syndrome baby. The chances of that woman having a Down's baby, regardless of whether or not she has already had such a child in the past, is about one in 300. But even the less risky of the two procedures pressed on middle-aged women by the NHS, chorionic villus sampling, will, in about one case in a hundred, produce a spontaneous abortion.

According to Dr Miriam Stoppard's *Pregnancy and Birth Book*— which is by no means hostile to these procedures—'very occasionally CVS may lead to rupture of the amniotic sac, infection and bleeding. Even so, the procedure only seems to increase the risk of miscarriage by 1 per cent.' Even so? Only 1 per cent? It is amazing that these facts are meant to reassure us. There is method in this madness, however. The NHS will provide, gratis, an abortion, if their tests show that the mother is expecting a Down's baby; an abortion even well after the normal legal limit of 24 weeks into the pregnancy, 'if there is a substantial risk that if the child were born it would suffer from such physical or mental abnormalities as to be seriously handicapped'.

This is nothing less than the state-sponsored annihilation of viable, sentient foetuses. In the People's Republic of China, the authorities wait until such children are born naturally, before starving them to death. In Hitler's Germany, even before the final solution to the Jewish 'problem', the Nazis were exterminating wholesale the mentally retarded. In this country the weeding-out process is done before birth, and only with the parents' consent. I do not think, however, that this constitutes a triumph for democracy.

Life Is Worth It

My life of disability has not been easy or carefree. [Hershey is severely disabled from a rare neuromuscular condition.] But in measuring the quality of my life, other factors—education, friends, and meaningful work, for example—have been decisive. If I were asked for an opinion on whether to bring a child into the world, knowing she would have the same limitations and opportunities I have had, I would not hesitate to say, "Yes."

Laura Hershey, *Ms.*, July/August 1994.

To the extent that this policy is more than half-baked eugenics, it is, to take the most charitable interpretation, based on the utilitarian idea that the child born with a physical or mental handicap will be an unhappy person, so unhappy that he or she would have been better off dead. One needs only to state this proposition to understand how presumptuous it is.

Not surprisingly I have, in the past week, been told by a number of well-meaning people that 'they'—meaning children with Down's syndrome—'are particularly happy people'. I have no idea if this is true, and I am inherently suspicious of such generalisations. But I see no reason why Domenica should be an unhappier person than her older sister, despite the extra chromosome which she has in her every cell.

Yet one or two acquaintances have still asked us, 'Didn't you have the tests?' My wife says she thinks it will be difficult to remain friends with such people. I think they are merely missing the point, although it is a very important point.

A Happy Life

Of all the letters which I have received since Domenica was born, perhaps the one which grasped this point best was from a fellow-atheist who wrote, after approving of our not 'having the tests': 'The reason why [such a decision] is admirable, of course, is that the sanctity of life is not just some obscure abstract principle. A life is a life, and every life can be filled with all kinds of positive things and real happiness—as I am sure your daughter's will be.'

At the moment, however, the happier of our children is the elder. She hated being the only child. Indeed she would often wail, heart-rendingly, 'I am so only! I am so only!' She is not only any more.

"[Abortion] is certainly the best solution in a case of rape."

Rape Justifies Abortion

Barbara Hernandez

Barbara Hernandez is the pseudonym of a woman who, in the following viewpoint, recounts the story of her rape by her brother-in-law, her subsequent pregnancy, and her decision to have an abortion. As a Catholic, she once believed abortion was murder; however, she now argues that abortion is a personal decision dictated by a woman's circumstances. Hernandez, now a teacher, maintains that aborting her pregnancy enabled her to return to a normal life and saved her sanity. The following viewpoint is taken from Hernandez's personal account, which is included in *Abortion—My Choice, God's Grace: Christian Women Tell Their Stories*, edited by Anne Eggebroten.

As you read, consider the following questions:

1. According to Hernandez, what reasons did her doctor give to assure her that rape justifies an abortion?
2. Why should abortion remain legal, in the author's opinion?

From Barbara Hernandez, "That Terrible Night," in *Abortion: My Choice, God's Grace: Christian Women Tell Their Stories*, edited by Anne Eggebroten, published by New Paradigm Books, PO Box 60008, Pasadena, CA 91116. Copyright ©1994 by Anne Eggebroten. Reprinted with permission.

That terrible night will haunt me for the rest of my life. On March 19, 1989, I went to San Antonio, Texas, on a business trip for a child development workshop. At the time I was a student at the University of Texas at Austin.

My married sister lived in San Antonio, so I decided to stay with her for the weekend. Arriving at her house, however, I found she had suddenly gone to my parents' home for the weekend. Only my brother-in-law was there, so I changed my mind. I would only stay overnight. I knew the workshop would finish late, and I didn't want to drive back to Austin alone at night.

When I got to my sister's after the child development meetings I was tired, but I decided to prepare dinner for my brother-in-law and me. After eating, I sat in the living room for a while watching television. My brother-in-law, Joe, thought I was bored and asked if there was any place I would like to go for a drink or dancing. I was very tired and decided to stay home. He still went out.

The Rape

Later that night, while I was in bed asleep, I heard a noise. Someone was opening the front door. Automatically I realized it was Joe, so I didn't get up to check, and fell back to sleep. I then heard the noise again. My bedroom door was opening and someone's tall shadow was standing there. I saw it was just Joe, so I relaxed, thinking he was getting something from the closet. Then I realized that he was approaching the bed. In that instant my eyes flew open and my heart started pumping fast. I was scared and confused about what he was up to. I asked him what was wrong. He answered that he wanted to be in bed with me. I could not believe my ears, but as soon as I realized what he had said, I jumped out of the bed and went toward the bedroom door. Before I reached it, he grabbed me and pushed me harshly on the bed.

I was frightened, screaming and crying and hoping some neighbor would hear my screams and come to help me. No one heard. Meanwhile my brother-in-law was struggling to take my clothes off. Because I was fighting back so hard, I was using up all my strength. I was kicking and hitting him and trying to get away, but he was so strong that nothing was successful. Still I kept fighting him back, but it made him more ferocious; he pushed me harder on the bed and took advantage of me. Joe attacked me sexually. I felt terrible—I just wanted to die.

When he was done, with the little strength I had left, I dragged myself out of the bed and ran into the bathroom and locked myself in. I was so frightened that I didn't want to come out and ended up staying there until I heard no noise in the house.

Finally I crept out cautiously, making sure Joe was not around.

In the bedroom I got dressed as fast as I could and ran out of the house so quickly I fell down the steps. I drove off and stopped at the nearest phone booth to call my brother. Because I was crying so hard, he could hardly understand me. I managed to get the story out. It took a few moments for him to absorb the shock. When he finally found his voice, I could feel his anger towards Joe as well as his sorrow for me.

Abortion Versus Adoption

Christina [who became pregnant after being raped] had heard the abortion foes' arguments for continuing a pregnancy resulting from rape. Rape is violent enough without having two victims instead of one, they said. The mother begins to heal from the attack with the child's birth. But Christina knew that as long as she was pregnant, she would feel vulnerable. And as guilty as she felt to be ridding herself of the life that grew within her, she came first. She wouldn't let the abortion foes get to her again. Losing a seven-week fetus which weighed less than an aspirin tablet didn't compare to losing [by giving up for adoption] a seven-pound wailing baby with hair and fingernails who looked just like her.

Sue Hertz, *Caught in the Crossfire*, 1991.

The night was beginning to fade into dawn and I still had to drive back to Austin. On my way back I kept getting flashbacks to the terror of that night. A few minutes after I reached my apartment, my brother arrived. He took me to the doctor and also took care of all the legal procedures for our brother-in-law to be punished for what he had done. He also informed my parents and my sister that I had been raped and by whom. What had happened was so hard and painful for everyone in my family to believe. Everyone felt anger and hatred toward Joe and concern about me.

Shocking News

I stayed in shock for several weeks, not only because of what had happened but also because of the doctor's later report. In the initial exam the doctor had performed a complete physical. I had been torn and bruised during the attack, but she wasn't sure whether I would have any long-term problems. When I returned to her office a few weeks later, she did another physical exam. This time the results were terrifying: I was pregnant. My heart stopped when she told me the news.

What a difficult position I was in. I had to make a decision on whether I was going to go through with this pregnancy. I was scared and confused because I believed that abortion was an immoral act, a sin. In fact, having been a Catholic all my life, I saw abortion as murder. I had not given the issue much thought, yet suddenly I had to decide whether I myself was to have an abortion.

Because of the circumstances of my rape, the doctor was totally against my continuing the pregnancy. She explained to me that in these circumstances I did not have to feel guilty if I chose an abortion. She presented it as a way to save my life, my sanity. It would not be murder. She was very clear that by no means should I go through with the pregnancy. She said that if I did, there would be chances of my not living a normal life because the flashbacks from my terrible experience would continue. Finally a joint decision was made by the doctor, my parents and me and an abortion was performed.

At first I felt guilty. I had ended a life that was just beginning. But gradually I realized that because of my circumstances, it was better for both the embryo and me.

I now believe that abortion is a decision that may come from a woman's unique set of circumstances. It is certainly the best solution in a case of rape or serious deformity. In my situation it was the answer. This is why the legal status of abortion must remain as it is. Because of my experience, I support the laws permitting abortion. It is up to the woman to evaluate her circumstances and determine whether she is to continue her pregnancy or terminate it. I had to make that decision.

"All children are gifts from God. It makes no difference how they are conceived."

Rape Does Not Justify Abortion

American Life League and Anonymous

In Part I of the following two-part viewpoint, the pro-life organization American Life League argues that rape does not justify abortion. Abortion only traumatizes the raped women further, the organization asserts, when the woman realizes she has killed her own child. A child resulting from a rape may help the woman recover from the experience. In Part II, an anonymous woman writes in a letter to the editor the story of her rape, her resulting pregnancy, and the birth of her daughter resulting from that rape. She contends that her baby is hers, not her rapist's. All life is sacred, the author maintains, and the manner of her daughter's conception is irrelevant.

As you read, consider the following questions:

1. When does life begin, in the opinion of the American Life League?
2. How common is pregnancy resulting from rape, according to the American Life League?
3. What reason does the anonymous woman give for choosing not to abort?

Part I: *Abortion—Not Even When the Pregnancy Is the Result of a Rape?*, pamphlet of the American Life League, Inc., ©1995. Reprinted with permission. Part II: "A Tremendous Story of Courage and Personal Triumph," Wanda Franz's column, Pro-Life Perspectives, *National Right to Life News*, April 24, 1995. Reprinted with permission.

I

Opponents of abortion rights walk a fine line when they con-
done any abortion. Based on their own definition, they are
guilty of being accessories to "murder" in certain circumstances by accepting rape and incest exceptions.

This quote from the Religious Coalition for Abortion Rights
(now the Religious Coalition for Reproductive Choice) shows
that even they recognize the inconsistency of making exceptions
to the pro-life position!

Human life begins at conception. Pro-life people take this fact
seriously, and understand it to mean—as it does mean—that the
person living inside the womb is as real as you or I. Therefore,
the preborn child must be treated equally, and be given the
same protection you and I enjoy under our Constitution.

What About Rape?

It is wrong to discriminate against people who have been born
because of the manner in which they came into the world, and
it is also wrong to discriminate against preborn people by attempting to justify abortion in cases where the mother has been
raped. Sadly, sometimes people who otherwise believe that the
preborn child deserves the right to life fail to see a preborn
child conceived through rape as fully human. An authentic pro-
life position rejects abortion in any circumstances!

A Closer Look

Why do some people believe abortion can be justified in the
case of rape? Some people believe in good faith that when rape
results in pregnancy, abortion can remove the painful evidence
of that rape. But will it?

Will abortion erase the memory of the rape or heal the emotional and physical pain of the assault? Will abortion, in effect,
erase the rape of a woman? Hardly. Rape is an act of violence
inflicted upon a woman. She is an innocent victim, and this
knowledge may someday help her come to terms with the rape
and rebuild her life. Abortion, on the other hand, is an act of violence that a mother inflicts on her own child. Through abortion, the mother becomes the aggressor, and this knowledge
may haunt her long after she has dealt with the rape.

Abortion only re-victimizes women who have been raped.
Anyone who thinks abortion is justified for rape victims should
consider the following:

This new human being, who is uniquely the mother's child,
may well be the only good—the only healing—that will come to
this woman from her rape experience. The woman deserves af-
firmation, love and time to recover from the assault. Her baby is

not a monster, and telling a woman that her best option is to get rid of her baby as soon as possible may only reinforce in her mind the idea that she is dirty, or a monster, herself.

In any pregnancy, the preborn child stimulates hormones in the mother's body to nurture the baby. These hormones often cause wide mood swings, which are especially influential to the mother who has been traumatized by rape and is aghast at the thought of being pregnant. The bonding between the mother and child that often occurs in pregnancy hasn't yet made the child seem "real" to the mother, real though the child is, and abortion seems to be a quick fix.

Conquering Rape

At a subconscious level, the rape victim feels that if she can get through the pregnancy she will have conquered the rape. Outlasting pregnancy shows she is better than the rapist who brutalized her. Giving birth, then, is the way rape victims seek to reclaim their self-esteem. It is a totally selfless act, a generous act, especially in light of the pressure to abort. It is a way for them to display their courage and strength to survive even a rape.

David C. Reardon, Human Life Alliance of Minnesota, Inc., advertising supplement, 1995.

Counselors who work with rape victims are familiar with the emotional trauma many women undergo as a result of rape. According to authors Sandra Makhorn and William Dolan, a woman often believes "that she is somehow tainted, dirty, and dehumanized" and knows "that many will see her either as pitiful and helpless or as disgusting and defiled." It has been reported that women who have had abortions often deal with exactly the same psychological symptoms as the rape victim: depression, guilt, low self-esteem, uncontrollable sadness and withdrawal.

The "quick fix" abortion "solution" is condescending and can only serve to reaffirm the sense of helplessness and vulnerability. Makhorn asserts that "Attitudes projected by others and not the pregnancy itself pose the central problem to the pregnant victim." When the trauma of rape is compounded by the trauma of abortion, it is hardly possible that abortion will lessen the emotional impact of the assault.

Many people mistakenly believe that pregnancy resulting from rape is very common. For a number of reasons, however, only a small number of women become pregnant as a result of sexual assault. Why? Many factors affect female fertility. Not only does age affect it, but so does a woman's natural cycle, which renders her able to conceive only approximately 4 to 6 days out of the month, and severe emotional trauma, which may prevent ovulation. Factors affecting male fertility include sexual dysfunction, and drug and alcohol use. It is estimated that, on average, only 0.49 percent—or one-half of one percent—of women who are raped become pregnant as a result.

It is a cruel irony that while a father cannot receive the death penalty for the crime of rape, his preborn child conceived in that rape can be executed without trial, jury or judge. Moreover, justice to the mother will not be achieved by sending her to the local abortion clinic to solve her problem. A mother's real needs must be met. Providing life-affirming medical, financial and emotional care meets these needs, and pro-life groups around the country—more than 2,900 crisis pregnancy centers, and groups like Life After Assault League—are doing this work.

The Point: No Exceptions

Pro-lifers are hypocrites if they condemn the murder of a preborn child in one circumstance but allow it in another. Think for a moment about your circle of friends. Can you tell just by looking at them how they were conceived? If one had been conceived in rape, would you treat him or her differently? Of course not. Regardless of how a life begins, each person is as valuable as the next. It is no different with preborn children's lives. They are valuable because they are human beings.

II

In response to [the] recent Letter to the Editor in which the writer stated that she does not believe that a child conceived during rape is a gift from God:

Consider my beautiful daughter, Jessica. She is eight months old, has no teeth but a full head of hair and seems to be developing a fondness for apple juice. She is loved by me, her grandparents, her uncle and her two sisters more than words can say.

She is also a child conceived during a rape.

I was raped in 1992. I did my civic duty and reported the rape. I worked with the assistant district attorney to prosecute my assailant. He was eventually pronounced "not guilty" because date rape is difficult to prove.

The Wrong Answer

When I discovered I was pregnant from the assault, I was horrified. I debated long and hard over what choice I should make.

Common sense would dictate that an abortion was the answer, right? Wrong. No matter how hideous my child's conception had been (and rape is a degrading, demoralizing act that alters one's whole life), I knew that there was a life growing inside me. I chose to accept this child as being my baby—not the rapist's. My friends and family supported me one-hundred percent, but the choice was mine to make and I know I made the right one.

All children are gifts from God. It makes no difference how they are conceived.

I feared I would see my rapist's face every time I looked at my child—but I don't. I see a beautiful, happy, little girl who wasn't planned and wasn't the result of an act of love—but nonetheless is loved very, very much.

In a perfect world, all babies would be wanted and conceived by loving couples. But the world we live in is a far cry from such an ideal. Violence abounds. People are mugged, murdered, robbed, and raped.

I don't consider my rape to be a gift from God, but my daughter is.

It was a difficult decision choosing not to abort. I based my decision upon the realization that I was already a victim of violence and knowing that I didn't want to make my unborn child another casualty.

All of those who believe abortion is justified in cases of rape should consider this: God truly does work in mysterious ways. My daughter, Jessica, is living proof of that.

Periodical Bibliography

The following articles have been selected to supplement the diverse views presented in this chapter. Addresses are provided for periodicals not indexed in the *Readers' Guide to Periodical Literature*, the *Alternative Press Index*, or the *Social Sciences Index*.

Kimberly A. Collins
"My Choice Was Pro-Me," *Essence*, March 1994.

Thomas E. Elkins and Douglas Brown
"Ethical Concerns and Future Directions in Maternal Screening for Down Syndrome," *Women's Health Issues*, Spring 1995. Available from Jacobs Institute of Women's Health, 409 Twelfth St. SW, Washington, DC 20024.

Glamour
"What Is an 'Undue Burden' in Seeking an Abortion?" September 1993.

Thomas Murphy Goodwin
"Medicalizing Abortion Decisions," *First Things*, March 1996. Available from PO Box 3000, Dept. FT, Denville, NJ 07834.

Laura Hershey
"Choosing Disability," *Ms.*, July/August 1994.

Nora Johnson
"Whose Life Is It?" *New York Times Magazine*, January 23, 1994.

David Liners
"Who Didn't Want Christina?" *Salt of the Earth*, November/December 1994. Available from 205 W. Monroe St., Chicago, IL 60606.

Judy Mann
"A Case of Terrible Choices," *Washington Post*, January 31, 1996. Available from Reprints, 1150 15th St. NW, Washington, DC 20071.

Caryl Rivers
"It's Not Just Victims of Rape and Incest," *Los Angeles Times*, December 11, 1991. Available from Reprints, Times Mirror Square, Los Angeles, CA 90053.

Sassy
"I Had My Rapist's Baby," November 1994.

Is Abortion Safe for Women?

Abortion

Chapter Preface

With an average of 1.5 million abortions performed every year since its legalization in 1973, abortion is the most common surgical procedure for women. Most medical professionals agree that the earlier an abortion is performed, the safer it is for the woman. Almost 90 percent of the women who obtain abortions are in their first trimester of pregnancy—less than 13 weeks pregnant. According to the National Abortion Federation (NAF), 97 percent of first-trimester abortions have no complications. "Abortion is the single safest surgical procedure there is," maintains Gina Shaw, director of communications at the NAF. "It's safer than a tonsillectomy, dental surgery, or even receiving a shot of penicillin." Deaths from legal abortion are extremely rare, according to the NAF; the organization reports one death for every 200,000 legal abortions performed. These deaths, Shaw maintains, are usually due to adverse reactions to anesthesia, heart attacks, or uncontrolled bleeding—risks that are associated with many other surgical procedures.

Abortion opponents disagree with the NAF's assessment of abortion's safety record, however. David Reardon, author of *Aborted Women: Silent No More*, argues that although the legalization of abortion has led to a lower risk of complication, it has also resulted in an increase in the number of women who have abortions. "This combination means that though the odds of any particular woman suffering ill effects from an abortion have dropped, the total number of women who suffer . . . from abortion is far greater than ever before," he asserts. Abortion opponents also contend that death rates from abortion are underreported. Mark Crutcher, an attorney for the pro-life legal firm Life Dynamics, maintains that the death certificates of many women who die during an abortion report the cause of death as an adverse reaction to anesthesia or as "complication due to maternity" rather than as due to the abortion procedure itself.

Abortion opponents and pro-choice activists disagree not only on the immediate safety of various abortion procedures but also on the long-term physical and psychological effects of abortion on women. The viewpoints in the following chapter debate the safety of the French abortion drug RU 486, whether women who have had abortions have a higher risk of developing breast cancer, and whether women suffer psychologically from abortions.

"Two of the [RU 486] pill's important attributes are its effectiveness and its safety."

RU 486 Is Safe for Women

Lawrence Lader

In the following viewpoint, Lawrence Lader argues that the drug known as RU 486 is an extremely safe method of abortion. He contends that most women who have experienced both surgical abortion and RU 486 abortion preferred the latter because it is a nonintrusive medical procedure. If used properly, RU 486 has no serious medical complications, he asserts, and therefore should not be denied to American women. Lader is the founding chair of the National Abortion and Reproductive Rights Action League. He is also the author of numerous books on abortion, including *RU 486* and *A Private Matter: RU 486 and the Abortion Crisis*, from which this viewpoint is taken.

As you read, consider the following questions:

1. In Lader's view, what are the advantages of an RU 486 abortion over a surgical abortion?
2. What are the disadvantages of an RU 486 abortion, according to the author?
3. What reason did the California Medical Association give for voting for the admission of RU 486 to the United States, as cited by Lader?

When the French government approved RU 486 for general use in September 1988, and the French minister of health hailed the new abortion pill as the "moral property of women," Abortion Rights Mobilization grasped its momentous consequences. ARM's board decided to concentrate on getting it into the United States. I decided to write a book titled *RU 486* to bring the pill's significance to the public. Here was a scientific advance that could eliminate the need for surgery, move the setting of abortion to the privacy of a doctor's office, and keep reproductive choice totally within the control of doctors and their patients. Opponents of abortion could not picket or raid every doctor's office in America. With clinics under a rising threat of firebombing, and clinic doctors targets of assassination, RU 486 had the potential of diminishing the furious clashes over abortion.

Safe and Effective

Two of the pill's important attributes are its effectiveness and its safety. It has induced abortion (followed by a dose of prostaglandin) in 96 percent of at least two hundred thousand cases. It has comparatively few side effects. It works by producing a heavy menstrual flow, virtually equivalent to a woman's normal period. There is no sign of an actual person, nothing resembling a possible finger or toe. It would be hard to differentiate the pill's action from a "miscarriage." An objective observer could scarcely claim that anything has been "killed." Referring to fetal tissue at this early stage, Dr. David Grimes, who ran early tests on RU 486 at the University of Southern California, explains, "You can't even find it."

It is hardly surprising that 77 percent of French women who have undergone both vacuum abortion and RU 486 abortion favored the pill. RU 486 has "de-medicalized" and humanized abortion. It eliminates what one French woman called "surgery aggression." Another pointed out, "There is no intrusion on the integrity of the body." An American woman in Dr. Grimes's tests concluded, "What I liked was taking care of myself, not being in the hands of doctors. It brought a sense of knowledge and control, a positive existential experience." RU 486 helps a woman feel that she is far more than flesh on a table subject to medical routine. It guarantees her sensitivity and makes her master of her life.

In contrast to the one-step process of vacuum abortion, RU 486 involves more time and complexities. In France the patient must be checked by a doctor to be certain her pregnancy is under seven weeks (nine weeks in Britain and elsewhere). Then the patient is given RU 486 (600 milligrams in one or more pills) and two days later a dose of prostaglandin to intensify the action. In the final visit, a medical exam confirms that abortion has been completed successfully and that bleeding has stopped.

The principal annoyances women experience from RU 486 combined with prostaglandin are uterine contractions, light nausea, and diarrhea, which may continue for a few hours. "Most women have no pain at all," concludes Dr. Elisabeth Aubeny in her French study. In a multinational study done by the World Health Organization, only 7.6 percent of the cases had enough pain to require narcotic analgesics. In a British study, 23 percent needed a painkiller.

Complications Are Rare

Medical complications from RU 486 have been rare. In France, two cardiovascular complications involved women thirty-five and thirty-eight years of age, one a heavy smoker, the other under severe psychological stress. Both women recovered completely. Doctors henceforth avoided giving the pill to older women, particularly to women with a predisposition to cardiovascular risks. Unfortunately, one French death has been attributed to RU 486. Statistically, every drug has a risk, and one death in over 200,000 RU 486 cases is a far lower rate than 1.1 deaths for 100,000 penicillin doses, which the public has been taking routinely for decades. Moreover, the patient was hypertensive and a heavy smoker and according to RU 486 standards should never have been accepted for treatment. With careful screening, such a tragic accident should never happen again.

A Safer Alternative

In places where sterilization of instruments is difficult, and trained medical personnel are overburdened, RU 486 may ultimately prove to be safer and less labor-intensive. . . . Anecdotal evidence from Brazil suggests that the unsupervised use of over-the-counter supplies of Cytotec, as a prostaglandin abortion inducer [used in conjunction with RU 486] has decreased complications from self-induced abortions significantly. Even under less than ideal conditions, RU 486 could save many lives.

Janet Callum and Rebecca Chalker, *Ms.*, March/April 1993.

It is a remarkable testament to the versatility of RU 486 that the compound not only has been used for abortion in France, Britain, Sweden (with U.S. tests now in progress [in 1995]), but that it may well become an important contraceptive. It could eliminate the possibility of pregnancy with a woman never knowing if she were pregnant or not. Another advantage is that as few as twelve doses a year may be the maximum required, thus limiting the impact on a woman's hormonal system, in contrast to about 240 doses of the present birth control pills. By inhibiting progesterone, RU 486 prevents preparation of the uterus for implantation of the egg.

A problem still to be solved involves the possibility of double-bleeding. A woman taking RU 486 as a contraceptive would not only bleed at that time but possibly again at the time of her normal end of cycle. Some researchers did not encounter this problem, and the chances of double-bleeding are greatly diminished by taking RU 486 two or three days before expected menses. Dr. Marc Bygdeman of the Karolinska Hospital in Stockholm, who initiated the research on combining prostaglandin with RU 486, concludes, "We think that if the pill is taken around twenty-four hours after ovulation it can prevent pregnancy."

Other Benefits

Already proven in European tests, RU 486 has become a critical factor in helping women through difficult deliveries. The drug may reduce the number of cesarean sections as an alternative for those deliveries. At least one of every four U.S. births seems to require a cesarean section. Because of its antiprogesterone effect, RU 486 makes the uterus contract and thus speeds the opening of the cervix.

In other aspects of delivery, RU 486 facilitates the extraction of ectopic embryos, abnormal fetuses, and fetuses that have died in the uterus. Further, RU 486 can be an essential supplement to late first trimester abortions done by the suction method. By dilating the cervix, it can diminish the breaking of muscle fibers and cervical damage, which sometimes results from the suction power of a vacuum machine or the internal probing of the machine's tube. Throughout the third trimester of pregnancy, RU 486 and prostaglandin may become an alternative to surgery to end a pregnancy as a result of a malformed fetus or because the mother's health is threatened. This therapy in late pregnancy could be generally less risky than the kinds of surgery now performed.

At the National Institutes of Health, located in Bethesda, Maryland, RU 486 has already proved valuable in treating Cushing's syndrome, a life-threatening condition that results from excessive production of the adrenal gland hormone cortisol and the abnormalities it causes in body tissue and blood chemistry. Surgery had always been the standard treatment.

But a National Institutes of Health report concludes:

> Surgery is particularly hazardous for patients with Cushing's syndrome, and the use of RU 486 to correct the abnormalities caused by excessive cortisol before surgery should make the procedure safer and improve outcome.

In another promising area of treatment, RU 486 has been used for meningioma, a primary tumor of the membrane that surrounds the brain and that often causes impaired mental function. "Brain tumors contain progesterone receptors," explains Dr. Daniel Philibert of the Roussel company, the French developer of the pill. Dr. Steven Grunberg of the University of Vermont reports that RU 486 "happens to have the hormonal effect that we're looking for to treat this tumor." After giving the compound to scores of patients, Grunberg concludes, "We're very excited and encouraged."

An Evolutionary Process

Like all scientific breakthroughs, RU 486 was the result of an evolutionary process, a chain of building blocks of research dating back many decades. It was the result of a research team at the Roussel company and the work on "receptors" by Dr. Étienne-Émile Baulieu, a professor at Bicêtre Hospital in Paris. The first insight came from one of Baulieu's mentors, Dr. Gregory Pincus, of the Worcester Foundation for Experimental Biology in Massachusetts, who theorized in 1962 that antiprogestins could act on specific receptors in the uterus and stop the growth of the egg. Baulieu had met Pincus the year before and was impressed by his research on the birth control pill.

Thirty years before, chemists had established the chemical structure of sex hormones or steroids, including estradiol, progesterone, and testosterone. But natural hormones from animals were inordinately expensive, and in the early 1940s, Professor Russell E. Marker of Pennsylvania State University discovered a far cheaper way to synthesize them. The newly formed Syntex company became the leading supplier of synthetic steroids. RU 486 is antagonistic to the sex hormone progesterone. By occupying the space in the progesterone receptor without activating it, RU 486 impedes progesterone from entering the receptor. Instead of inducing the usual hormone responses, RU 486 stops them.

Progesterone plays a central role in establishing pregnancy. It prepares the uterus for implantation and nurtures the egg. A specific receptor in the uterus receives the progesterone. If fertilization occurs, progesterone production helps the new embryo lodge in the lining of the uterus, promotes development of the placenta, and decreases the chance of expulsion of the embryo. RU 486 thus "barricades" the receptor. When RU 486 penetrates the receptor, it binds to it and deceives it, working against implantation. The developing placenta and embryo detach from the uterine lining. There are increased contractions that dislodge and expel the embryo. Through the seventh to ninth weeks of the woman's cycle, RU 486 brings about an early abortion because of diminished progesterone and bleeding that results from shedding of the endometrium (the mucous membrane lining the uterus).

When Baulieu started progesterone receptor research around 1970, no one knew how the receptor really functioned. A research group at Roussel headed by Dr. Georges Teutsch was trying to develop the best molecule close to cortisone (fortunately similar to progesterone), a molecule that would bind to and block the receptors without triggering the normal hormonal response. A steroid or sex hormone is like a key, and an antisteroid can prevent the key from opening the lock. Whereas Teutsch and his group were making a fake key that would fit the lock, Baulieu's work was defining the shape of the lock. By occupying the lock, a fake key would impede the real key from opening the door.

The Medical Benefits of RU 486

RU-486 is only in the body briefly, so the chance of long-lasting side effects is low. More than 10 years of clinical study and use in Europe have shown no long-term complications. . . .

RU-486 also has medical benefits unrelated to its contraceptive uses. It has been shown to reduce pain among women with endometriosis and to shrink uterine tumors. And it may be a potent treatment for breast cancer.

Marion Asnes, *Working Woman*, November 1994.

In a 1975 paper, Baulieu urged more research on the "relationship between receptor concentration and hormone action." Over the next few years, Teutsch tested hundreds of compounds. "We wanted one with the highest binding qualities," he recalled. All told, nine hundred compounds may have been screened. In 1980, Teutsch told a meeting of Roussel executives that some compounds had real potential as a new abortifacient. The compound Roussel finally decided to promote was called mifepristone, or RU 486. The company applied for a patent in 1980, and it was approved the next year.

Baulieu approached Professor Walter Hermann of Geneva's University Hospital, an old friend, and got him to search for female volunteers. Eleven pregnant women agreed to participate in the first test, and nine aborted quickly. In a test sample of a hundred women in 1986, RU 486 achieved a success rate of 85 percent. As an international network of scientists, including the World Health Organization, set up their own test programs, Dr. Bygdeman in Stockholm demonstrated that a small dose of prostaglandins (substances in body tissue that act like hormones) would make the uterus react more strongly than would RU 486 alone. Bleeding would be decreased. Abortion often occurred within a few hours. As a result of the combined dosages, the success rate was quickly raised to 96 percent. Studies showed that no other receptors were affected except for a weak anticortisone action. Consequently, women have been able to conceive again shortly after undergoing an RU 486 abortion.

"RU 486 . . . has injured and even killed women."

RU 486
Is Not Safe
for Women

Randall K. O'Bannon

The drug RU 486, taken in combination with prostaglandin, can be used to abort a pregnancy up to the ninth week. In the following viewpoint, Randall K. O'Bannon argues that these powerful drugs have side effects that are dangerous for women. RU 486 abortions are more painful and bloody than the drug's promoters acknowledge, he maintains. Furthermore, O'Bannon contends that RU 486 abortions may be psychologically devastating for many women because they can see the results of the abortion. O'Bannon is the director of research for the National Right to Life Committee.

As you read, consider the following questions:

1. How does RU 486 cause an abortion, in O'Bannon's view?
2. What are some of the side effects women experience during an RU 486 abortion, according to the author?
3. In O'Bannon's opinion, what is the real reason abortion advocates want RU 486 accepted as an abortion method?

From Randall K. O'Bannon, "RU 486," *National Right to Life News*, January 1995. Reprinted with permission.

Among the numerous proabortion initiatives undertaken by the Clinton Administration, few were pushed any harder than the vigorous attempt to bring the abortifacient RU 486 into the United States.

As part of a payback to his proabortion supporters, newly inaugurated President Bill Clinton took only three days to order Department of Health and Human Services (DHHS) Secretary Donna Shalala to "promptly assess initiatives by which the DHHS can promote the testing, licensing, and manufacturing in the United States of RU 486."

Yet there were (and remain) many unanswered questions about this two-drug abortion technique. Thus, even though Food and Drug Administration (FDA) Commissioner David Kessler announced only three months later [April 1993] that an agreement had been reached to license RU 486 for U.S. distribution, it took another year to consummate that agreement with the French manufacturer of RU 486, Roussel Uclaf. . . .

On May 15, 1994, Roussel Uclaf and the Population Council reached an agreement purportedly transferring the U.S. patent rights and all technology, free of charge, to the New York–based Population Council. . . .

The FDA has announced that it would accept foreign testing data (largely compiled by researchers with some tie to Roussel Uclaf), something not commonly done. This not only saves the Population Council millions of dollars but also moves up the target approval date to sometime in 1996. Normally, the company seeking FDA approval for a new drug has to spend an average of four to five years testing the drug, at a cost somewhere in the neighborhood of well over $100 million.

If ever the FDA had reason to turn down a drug, this qualifies. RU 486 kills an unborn baby whose heart has already begun to beat by starving the baby to death and has injured and even killed women. No matter what other theoretical potential benefits (treatment of some breast cancers, brain tumors, etc.) its promoters offer to try to soften the drug's image, its only real purpose, and the only use it has ever been licensed for, is to kill unborn babies.

How RU 486 Works

RU 486 blocks the hormone progesterone, which helps to create and maintain the uterine lining which provides nourishment for the developing child. RU 486 molecules fill the hormone receptor sites normally filled by progesterone in a healthy pregnancy. The uterus never gets the "message" to maintain the pregnancy. Deprived of the food she needs to grow and develop as the lining of the uterus begins to decay and slough off, the unborn child usually shrivels and finally starves to death.

However, at least 15% of the time, RU 486, used alone, "fails" to result in a complete abortion. To increase the "kill ratio," it has become standard procedure to supplement RU 486 with a second drug, an artificial prostaglandin (typically Cytotec) taken two days later. The synthetic prostaglandin stimulates stronger contractions to insure the expulsion of the embryo and the rest of the uterine contents.

Even when these two drugs are taken together, the rate of "successful" abortion is only about 95% (some studies put the number closer to 90%). Doctors administering RU 486 urge patients who don't abort after ingesting this "chemical cocktail" to have a surgical abortion to avoid possibly giving birth to a child with gross malformations due to the two powerful drugs' effect on the developing human embryo.

Serious Complications

That RU 486 causes a helpless, innocent, developing unborn child to starve to death is reason enough to ban its use. But the effect of these toxic chemicals on the women who take them is yet another reason to keep these deadly drugs off the market.

Even when used under close medical supervision, women using the RU 486/prostaglandin combination often experience a host of troubling side effects: severe pain, nausea, fatigue, vomiting, excessive thirst, and heavy bleeding. These are just the most common side effects. There have also been documented cases of heart attacks and even death.

The latest strategy of the promoters of RU 486 is to admit some of the more common side effects, but to downplay the pain, nausea, and bleeding by telling women it is not more than might be expected during a "heavy period." But this is hardly supported by the results of the early American trials.

In its December 5, 1994, edition, *Time* described the RU 486/Cytotec abortion technique as a "painful, messy, and protracted" procedure. The first patient to take the combination in Des Moines told *Time*, "I was very nauseous in a couple of hours. I threw up constantly for three days. . . . It was like food poisoning. I couldn't keep anything down."

And the bleeding? After taking the prostaglandin (the second drug), the woman reported that "I went to the restroom. When I started to stand up, it was like a faucet turned on. There was a steady stream of blood. I passed a golf-ball size blood clot that scared me. I thought maybe it was the fetus.

"The cramps stayed steady. In the last 15 minutes of my appointment, I was doubled over. The bleeding was very heavy, heavier than a period. My mom drove me home. By this time, I was bleeding severely, and I had diarrhea." The workers at the Des Moines Planned Parenthood clinic had told her she was "making history."

While beginning to admit the unavoidable truth that RU 486/prostaglandin abortions are bloody and painful (and in doing so hoping to pass these off as normal), those pushing these drugs usually fail to mention that the pain is often so severe that as many as 30% require narcotic analgesics (according to the British manufacturer of RU 486). The bleeding, which itself may last from 10 to 40 days, is so severe that one out of every 100 actually require transfusions. Hardly "minor complications," certainly not "safe" and "simple."

© Cullum/Copley News Service. Reprinted with permission.

And then there are the heart attacks, the uterine ruptures, and death. The response of researchers (naturally, after the fact) to these more serious dangers had been to issue recommendations that certain women not be allowed to take the drug. So far, use of the drug has been put off limits to women under 18 and over 35, women less than five or more than nine weeks' pregnant, smokers, women with high blood pressure, women who are obese, diabetic, asthmatic, suffering from colitis or ulcers, having irregular menstrual cycles, etc. The list is sure to grow, since so little is known about how RU 486 really operates and new glitches seem to be found every day.

Long-term physical effects still haven't really been studied. For example, RU 486 crosses the blood follicle barrier and has been found in the egg follicles of women taking the drug. How this might affect future fertility, pregnancy, and the health of future children is not yet known. Yet proponents still blithely offer assurances of RU 486's safety.

As an artificial hormone, RU 486 interacts with a host of other hormone receptor sites scattered throughout the body. The action of RU 486, while certainly deadly to the unborn child, is not specific to abortion alone, and still may prove toxic in many other ways.

Not only does RU 486 block the work of progesterone, but, because of its similar chemical structure, it also blocks the normal activity of cortisol, a hormone crucial to many of the body's metabolic, nervous, and circulatory functions. While most progesterone receptor sites are found in various organs of the female reproductive system, every tissue of the body binds cortisol, theoretically opening every system of the body to RU 486's toxic effects.

Not only does RU 486 linger in all the body's tissues for several days, but it is also absorbed into the cells in the area where RNA and DNA are stored. What effects this has on a woman's DNA or RNA is unknown. But phenyl, an important part of the RU 486 molecule, is known to be a toxic substance for humans.

Just how little they know about the workings of RU 486 and just how little that lack of knowledge has bothered the producers of RU 486 was made clear by a statement of Etienne Emile Baulieu, the French researcher widely known as the "father of the abortion pill." Commenting on the role RU 486 plays in the gene transcription process in the uterus, Baulieu wrote in his book *The Abortion Pill*, "How lucky we were not to know of this complexity before testing RU 486, which worked so well on the basis of a simple hypothesis!" The troubling thing is that despite its clear lack of understanding about RU 486 and how it interacts with the body, Roussel has had no qualms declaring it safe.

In a country where thousands already suffer from post-abortion syndrome (PAS) and millions more are at latent risk, the psychological fallout from RU 486 abortions is likely to be staggering. Unlike a typical surgical abortion where the woman is shielded from the sight of her bloody, dismembered baby, women taking RU 486 actually see their aborted children. *Time* quotes the account of an RU 486 patient participating in the Des Moines trial: "I was having deep cramping when I went to the bathroom, and it was like turning a water jug upside down. I looked at the fetus and was disgusted. I flushed before I got sick to my stomach."

Other accounts have shown her experience is not atypical. According to the *New York Times*, two RU 486 patients selected by the Population Council to appear at its October 27, 1994, press conference "agreed that some women who wanted to remain unaware of when the embryo was flushed out of the body would not like the procedure."

Even the then-president of Roussel Uclaf admitted in an interview published in the August 1, 1990, edition of *Le Monde* that an RU 486 abortion is "an appalling psychological ordeal." And this just refers to a woman's immediate psychological response. Given the horrible dreams that plague some sufferers of PAS, one can only shudder to think what nightmares will someday visit those who actually saw the tiny, emaciated bodies of their own abortion children.

The RU 486 Agenda

Though advocates of RU 486 claim they merely want to replace surgical abortions with chemical ones, the truth is that RU 486 is part of a concerted effort to expand abortion services throughout the United States.

The vast majority of abortions performed in the United States today are done at free-standing abortion facilities. Proponents hope that the onset of RU 486 will enable them to turn every willing Ob-Gyn [obstetrician-gynecologist] into an abortionist. There are indications that the number of Ob-Gyns willing to prescribe RU 486 may be considerable. A recent survey of 466 obstetricians and gynecologists from California found almost a third (32%) of the physicians initially saying they were unwilling to perform abortions later saying they would do so if RU 486 became available.

If such figures hold true nationwide, abortion will be coming to many communities where it has not been welcome. *And more abortionists and more locations mean more abortions.*

There will be more abortions for another reason. Quite frankly, many women repulsed or frightened at the prospect of a surgical abortion will hear the propaganda about a "simple, safe, natural" alternative and choose to chemically abort babies they might have carried to term. The *Time* magazine article confirms this scenario.

Women told *Time* they considered "taking pills" "a lot less traumatic" than surgical abortions. One 19-year-old said, "I didn't like abortion and said I'd never have one. These were just pills."

One of the women said she "was terrified of a surgical abortion because of a friend's bad experience." She had always told herself "I could never do that [have an abortion]." But when she heard of RU 486 and found herself pregnant, she decided to participate in the Des Moines trial.

If RU 486 had not been available, not only would these women have avoided the awful effects of those chemicals on their bodies, but their babies might still be alive today.

"The best evidence for the real existence of a link between induced abortion and breast cancer is that it has been repeatedly observed in so many studies."

Abortion Increases a Woman's Risk of Breast Cancer

Joel Brind

Numerous studies show that women who have had abortions have an increased risk for breast cancer, maintains Joel Brind in the following viewpoint. According to Brind, the 50 percent risk increase revealed by the studies means that women face a higher risk of eventually dying from the effects of an abortion than of dying in childbirth. Researchers and reporters who discount the elevated risk of breast cancer are pawns of the "pro-choice" movement, he contends, whose sole aim is to convince the public that abortion is safe. Brind is a professor of biology and endocrinology at Baruch College of the City University of New York.

As you read, consider the following questions:

1. How does the response-bias hypothesis affect studies linking abortion and breast cancer, as cited by the author?
2. What is the best evidence of a real link between abortion and breast cancer, in the author's opinion?
3. According to Brind, how does carrying a pregnancy to term protect a woman against breast cancer?

From Joel Brind, "May Cause Cancer," *National Review*, December 25, 1995; ©1995 by National Review, Inc., 150 E. 35th St., New York, NY 10016. Reprinted by permission.

On November 4, 1994, the *Journal of the National Cancer Institute* (NCI) published a study that the media have treated as an unscientific scare story, the way they should have treated the Alar and PCB cancer scares of years past. The study, by Dr. Janet Daling, et al., found a significant overall increase in breast cancer among Washington State women who had had one or more induced abortions (as opposed to spontaneous abortions, or miscarriages, which were not associated with increased risk).

The spin doctoring began immediately—and not just in the popular media, but in the professional medical press. In fact, even as the Daling study rolled off the press, it was undercut by an accompanying editorial warning that "neither a coherent body of knowledge nor a convincing biologic mechanism has been established." Articles critical of the study continued to appear well into the summer of 1995.

Not an Isolated Study

To be sure, one ought to be extremely wary of raising public fears on the basis of any one study in isolation. This is especially important when one is considering such a high-incidence, potentially lethal disease as breast cancer (now estimated to strike about 12 per cent of American women), and such a high-incidence posited risk factor as induced abortion (over 1.5 million a year). If even the modest 50 per cent overall risk increase found in the NCI study holds up, that would result in 40,000 to 50,000 additional cases of breast cancer a year, once the post–*Roe v. Wade* cohort starts to reach the age range at which breast cancer becomes more likely. Clearly, the fears engendered by such a study would affect a great many people.

On the other hand, if the study *does* prove valid, it is important to note that the posited risk factor is almost exclusively a matter of personal choice, and therefore avoidable in a way that environmental risk factors may not be.

In this case, however, the study is not isolated. Evidence of a possible connection between abortion and breast cancer has been published quietly since as far back as 1957.

The attack on the Daling study began, as I say, with a debunking editorial in the same issue of the NCI *Journal*, written by Boston epidemiologist Lynn Rosenberg. Her own work in the field, published by the *American Journal of Epidemiology*, was seriously flawed because the breast-cancer patients in her study were, on average, 12 years older than the cancer-free control patients. Since the risk of cancer increases with age, this was an egregious methodological error. Not surprisingly, her study evidenced a relative risk (RR) of breast cancer among women who had had one or more induced abortions of only 1.2 to 1.3 (i.e., a 20 to 30 per cent elevation in risk). This risk increase was reported as not statistically significant.

Perhaps that explains why her study was publishable in an American medical journal. The same *American Journal of Epidemiology* declined to publish an age-matched study of New York State women by Dr. Holly Howe, et al., of New York State's own Department of Health, a study which found a significant relative risk (RR) of 1.9 for breast cancer among women who had had any induced abortions. The Howe study was finally published in the *English International Journal of Epidemiology* in 1989.

The Response-Bias Hypothesis

While the *American Journal of Epidemiology* did not publish the Howe study, it did (in 1991) publish a comparison of studies done in Sweden which claimed to "explain the tendency toward increased risk of breast cancer which . . . appears to be associated with induced abortion" by a hypothesis called "response bias." According to this hypothesis, can-er-free women are more likely to deny abortions they had, while women with breast cancer are more likely to report their abortion history accurately. While the response-bias hypothesis is plausible and worthy of testing, the only evidence the study provided was that breast-cancer patients reported abortions of which the computer had no record. It is on this that the 1991 paper bases its assertion that patients tend to "overreport abortions"—that is, to imagine abortions they never had.

Breast Cancer Rates Increase with Abortion

Jewish women are considered to be at higher risk for breast cancer than the general population. Could that be because many Jews have a permissive attitude toward abortion? Or consider the case of the old Soviet Union. Women in the U.S.S.R. had difficulty gaining access to contraceptives, but abortion was widely available. Between 1960 and 1987, the rate of breast cancer among Russian, Estonian and Georgian women tripled.

After Washington state began to provide public funding for abortions in 1970, the breast cancer rate among the poor rose by 53 percent, while the rate for rich women dropped by 1 percent.

Mona Charen, *Conservative Chronicle*, November 2, 1994.

Despite the absurdity of this evidence, the response-bias argument was mobilized to attack the Daling-NCI study. Harvard epidemiologist Karin Michels reported it to the *New York Times* as fact when the Daling study came out: "That [i.e., patient-recall-based data collection] is a flaw in the study design because women who had breast cancer are more likely to disclose an abortion than women who did not develop breast cancer." Lynn Rosenberg, in her editorial, suggested "the possibility of reporting bias" as a "limitation" of "major concern" in the Daling study, even though the Daling study itself soundly debunks the reporting-bias theory. So did the Howe study: while it revealed some misreporting of prior induced abortions either as being spontaneous abortions or as not having occurred at all, it also revealed that the misreporting "occurred similarly among the cases and the controls."

International Studies

The first study (in 1957) to show a significant association between induced abortion and breast cancer (relative risk = 2.6) was performed and published in Japan, and subsequent reports with similar results were also published overseas. Another large, age-matched Japanese study (1982) showed risk to rise steadily with the number of induced abortions (RR = 2.5 for one abortion, up to 4.9 for four or more). American studies showing significant risk increases among women on the West Coast (1981; RR = 2.4 for abortion terminating a first pregnancy) and on the East Coast (the 1989 Howe study) were published in England. Similar findings from France (1984; RR = 1.2 for one abortion, 1.6 for two or more), Denmark (1988; RR = 3.9 for abortion terminating a first pregnancy), and the former Soviet Union (1978; RR = 1.7 for any abortion) also popped up in European journals. In addition to the 10 epidemiological studies cited thus far, another 12 case-control studies have appeared in the peer-reviewed medical literature. Four (two in the United States and one each in France and Italy) showed no overall trend of increased risk (RR = 0.9 to 1.1); three (one in America and two in Japan) showed risk elevations that did not achieve statistical significance (RR = 1.2, 1.5, and 1.5, respectively); and four recent studies showed significant risk elevations, two in American women (RR = 1.23 and 3.1), one in Greek women (RR = 1.51), and one in Dutch women (RR = 1.9). In fact, the only case-control study showing a negative association between induced abortion and breast cancer was a 1979 Yugoslavian study which was atypical in other ways as well. For example, it showed no evidence of the universally recognized protective effect of having children. . . .

Pregnancy's Benefit

The first trimester of a normal pregnancy is marked by a surge of hormones from the mother's ovaries, including progesterone, to maintain the pregnancy, and estrogen, which makes the breasts grow. Most known breast-cancer risk factors act via some form of overexposure to estrogen. Normally, the high estrogen levels of early pregnancy are counterbalanced by other hormones late in the pregnancy, which differentiate the breasts into milk-producing organs, thus rendering them permanently less susceptible to cancer. However, if the pregnancy is artificially terminated, the growth-stimulating effects of the estrogen surge help primitive and/or abnormal cells to grow into potential cancers. Contrariwise, as more than twenty years of research have shown, most first-trimester spontaneous abortions are characterized by subnormal secretion of ovarian hormones, including estrogen, whether because of inadequate stimulation by an abnormal fetus or because of an inadequate response by abnormal ovaries. Clearly, the failure to distinguish between spontaneous and induced abortion is a fatal weakness in any study.

Other confounding variables, such as socioeconomic class, race/ethnicity, and diet may also contribute to apparent increases in breast-cancer risk, and these are controlled for (sometimes well and sometimes not so well) by the selection of an appropriate control group. All in all, the best evidence for the real existence of a link between induced abortion and breast cancer is that it has been repeatedly observed in so many studies in different countries of widely varying ethnicity, diet and other lifestyle factors, and baseline breast-cancer incidence, and over a time span of almost four decades.

A Wall of Silence

The American medical media's wall of silence on the possible link between abortion and breast cancer was first breached in December 1993 in the African-American *Journal of the National Medical Association*. As Dr. Amelia Laing, et al., noted in the introduction to their age-matched Howard University study of over 1,000 black women, "Breast cancer is the leading cause of cancer mortality in black women," and "among women under the age of 50, the mortality rate in whites has declined, while it has increased in blacks." Thus (with black women also heavily overrepresented among abortion clients) there was a compelling interest in publishing their findings of significantly elevated risk among black women with any induced abortions (RR = 2.7), risk which steadily rose with age until it reached 4.7 in the fifty-and-over group (which made up the majority of the study population).

The Howard University study was ignored by the mainstream popular press. Even the *Philadelphia Inquirer*, which heralded the Daling-NCI study, made no mention of the Howard study in a 3,000-word feature story on breast cancer in black women, written two months after the Daling-NCI story. . . .

One needn't look very far to find the motivation behind the

increasingly desperate attempts to prevent public access to the considerable body of evidence of a connection between induced abortion and breast cancer: the reputation of abortion as safe for women is crucial to the "pro-choice" movement. The American Medical Association staunchly maintains that the risk of dying in childbirth is 12 times greater than the risk of dying from an abortion. Now, the risk of dying in childbirth is less than 5 in 100,000. If the overall increase in breast-cancer risk caused by induced abortion is even the modest 50 per cent suggested by numerous studies, that would raise lifetime risk from 12 per cent to 18 per cent—an increased incidence of 6,000 per 100,000 women who have had any abortions. Even with a breast-cancer cure rate of 75 per cent, the increase in the death rate from induced abortion would calculate out to 1,500 per 100,000, making abortion 300 times more likely to result in death to a woman than childbirth. But mentioning that would be *very* un-PC.

"A 50% increase in their relative risk of breast cancer . . . would still be small in comparison with other, well-established risk factors."

The Increased Risk of Breast Cancer from Abortion Is Insignificant

The Economist

Many medical studies have shown that a woman's reproductive history affects her risk of breast cancer. In the following viewpoint, the *Economist*, a British weekly magazine, maintains that the risks associated with abortion are insignificant compared with other well-documented breast cancer risks, such as alcohol consumption and weight. Moreover, the *Economist* contends, studies on the link between breast cancer and abortion have reached contradictory conclusions. More research is needed to determine if abortion actually presents a risk for breast cancer, the *Economist* concludes.

As you read, consider the following questions:

1. Why has the breast cancer rate risen from 830 to 1,370 cases per million American women, according to the *Economist*?
2. According to the author, what is the problem with Janet Daling's study linking abortion with breast cancer?
3. In the *Economist*'s view, why do studies concerning abortion sometimes result in contradictory conclusions?

Until the twentieth century, nuns were more likely than other women to get breast cancer. They still get it. But so, especially in the West, do thousands of their secular sisters. The reason, like the reason for the parallel increase in cancer of the lung, is environmental. But unlike lung cancer, which is due to the presence of cigarette smoke, breast cancer is often due to the absence of something: babies.

Medical studies have shown again and again that not reproducing is bad for the breasts. In particular, a woman's age of first menstruation and her age at the birth of her first child are important risk factors. The earlier the former and the later the latter, the greater the risk. And since improved nutrition has caused the age of first menstruation to fall, and improved contraception and changed female career patterns have caused the age of first birth to rise, it is no surprise that the rate of breast cancer has increased from 830 to 1370 cases per million American women since 1973.

Abortion and Breast Cancer

So much is widely accepted. However, it is now being suggested by some anti-abortion campaigners in America that another form of non-reproduction can give you breast cancer: abortion.

The basis for this claim appears to be a study published late in 1994 by Janet Daling and her colleagues at the Fred Hutchinson Cancer Research Centre in Seattle. Dr Daling's results suggested that, among women who had been pregnant at least once, those who had had an abortion were at a 50% greater risk of getting breast cancer than those who had not. At particular risk, according to Dr Daling, were those whose abortions had happened when they were under 18.

This is not, in itself, implausible. Most under-18 abortions happen to women who have never given birth. The breasts of women who have not had a child are not fully formed. Although a woman's breasts go through an initial burst of growth at puberty, the tissues then enter a sort of suspended animation until her first pregnancy. Once that pregnancy begins, the breast cells start to multiply again, under the influence of a hormone, progesterone.

Multiplying cells are a significant cancer risk (cancers are, after all, just masses of proliferating cells that do not know when to stop). Indeed, this seems to be the reason why not reproducing can help induce cancer. The incomplete breast tissues are susceptible to the hormone fluctuations that go on during each menstrual cycle. These stimulate a little bit of cell multiplication each month. The more months between the formation of the breasts and their completion by pregnancy, the greater the

162

risk that, one day, the multiplication could get out of hand. So, the hypothesis goes, if the cell multiplication that comes with first pregnancy is not allowed to reach its conclusion it, too, might help lead to cancer.

Not implausible. But on the basis of Dr Daling's study, not proven. Her result was based on the fact that 20 of her breast-cancer patients had had abortions before they were 18, but only 15 members of the control group had done so—a barely significant difference. Besides, even if it were true that women who have had abortions have a 50% increase in their relative risk of breast cancer, as the study suggests, the increase would still be small in comparison with other, well-established risk factors, such as body weight and alcohol consumption.

No Increase Found in Breast Cancer Rate

It's not uncommon for a woman in Japan to have had 10 or more abortions. But Japan has the world's lowest breast-cancer rate.

In the United States, the highest breast-cancer rate is among women over 65, who generally haven't had many abortions. Women under 45 show no major recent increase, even though they're more likely to have had an abortion.

Devra Lee Davis, *Washington Post*, March 14, 1995.

But it is probably not true. Dr Daling studied 845 women who had suffered breast cancer. She compared them with 961 non-sufferers. These look like large numbers. But epidemiological studies of this sort have a common problem. There are so many variables to consider that, once the sample has been parcelled out into categories such as "women who have had an abortion before the age of 18, and also had breast cancer", the individual numbers may be barely large enough for meaningful statistical testing. At the least, they need careful interpretation. More importantly, they need replication in other studies.

Further Research Is Needed

This is not to criticise Dr Daling, who points out clearly that many of those other studies (there have been several dozen) come to other, sometimes opposite, conclusions. She merely calls for further research to clarify the matter. Such contradictory results are common in epidemiology, unless either the original sample, or the effect, is huge. But workers in this area of research face an added difficulty. People lie, particularly about their sex lives, and particularly about procedures such as abortion that have a stigma attached to them. Studies have shown that they are more likely to lie if they are healthy. And, it seems, they particularly lie if asked orally rather than in writing. Dr Daling conducted her research face to face.

Further evidence of this reluctance to tell the truth has just been unearthed by Polly Newcomb (who also works at the Fred Hutchinson Centre) and her colleagues. Dr Newcomb's results, the product of interviews carried out over the telephone, were published in January 1996 in the *Journal of the American Medical Association*. Superficially, they support Dr Daling: all other things being equal, women who had had abortions had a 23% higher rate of cancer than those who had not. But the results depended strongly on whether a woman's abortion took place before or after it was legal. The particular legal regime applying at any moment is unlikely, even with back-street abortionists, to influence a disease such as breast cancer.

Women whose abortions were carried out before 1973 had a 35% increased risk. After 1973 this dropped to 12%. The most likely explanation of these results is that many of the healthy "pre-1973ers" were lying about their lack of abortions—they had, after all, been guilty of a crime. Given which, it is plausible that the "post-1973ers" were also lying, albeit less, over what was still an embarrassing, even if not an illegal, act.

All of this suggests that while such studies may not have demonstrated a clear link between breast cancer and abortion, they have shown a need for a more reliable way of investigating the problem. If a link exists, selective use of the data, and scare campaigns mounted on the basis of such selection, will not find it. By adding to the fear and stigma, they will just make the job of researchers harder still.

"[After the abortion], I fall into a period of despair. I stop seeing friends. . . . When I am not in despair, I feel nothing."

Post-Abortion Syndrome Harms Women

Madelein Gray

Anti-abortion advocates contend that many women are traumatized after their abortions when they realize they have killed their babies. The advocates assert that this trauma, known as post-abortion syndrome (PAS), is a common reaction to abortion. In the following viewpoint, Madelein Gray recounts her own feelings of despair, depression, and alienation after aborting her fourth pregnancy. Gray maintains that she did not begin to heal from PAS until she accepted God's forgiveness. Madelein Gray is the pseudonym of a freelance writer in Wisconsin.

As you read, consider the following questions:

1. What reason does the author give for avoiding abortion counselors with a pro-life bias?
2. According to Gray, why is she telling the story of her abortion?
3. How can the church help more women who have had abortions, in Gray's opinion?

Madelein Gray, "Giving Up the Gift," *Commonweal*, February 25, 1994; © 1994 by Commonweal Foundation. Reprinted with permission.

Until I crashed against my limitations, I seemed to be the perfect Catholic mother. I was known as an active parishioner and eucharistic minister who had borne three children despite a serious chronic illness. I cherished them as signs of grace and kept these lively children at the center of my life. Though I often felt drained, I welcomed the possibility of a fourth child someday.

When I actually became pregnant again, an astonishingly intense depression, along with further deterioration of my health, led to an abortion. Nearly three years later, I am still appalled by what I have done. I still mourn my baby and my former idea of who I was. My grief is compounded by my estrangement from my church.

I do not wish to grieve silently any longer, partly because I realize that I have many co-mourners. It is horrifying to realize that a million-and-a-half uniquely painful stories are played out each year in the United States. But the real women behind the statistics rarely tell their stories. In the abortion debate, this public battle about the most personal of matters, the voices left unheard, the stories lost among the placards and drowned out by simplistic slogans are those of the very women who have felt desperate enough to seek abortion.

If we are Catholic, we are afraid of being shamed and hurt even more than we already are. We fear we would be accused of being selfish and thoughtless. Wounded as we are, we remain silent, alone, unreconciled.

I am intensely aware of the precious gift a baby is. I have Crohn's disease, which causes chronic inflammation and ulceration of the digestive tract. The illness flares without pattern or warning, sometimes leaving me gravely ill, feverish, and weak. During each of my pregnancies I had to take potent steroid medications to restore my health and prayed that my baby would be all right. . . .

Making the Decision

December 1990—I am shocked to find out I am pregnant for the fourth time. In a romantic moment during a "safe" time of the month we had let our better judgment lapse. It was human failure, pure and simple.

I am even more shocked by my reaction. I fall into a deep depression. It is so hard to face reality that I literally spend days in bed under a heap of blankets, coming out from under them only when absolutely necessary. Life was such a precarious balance already. How can we handle a fourth child?

I have the awful feeling that I am losing my three children. They are still so young—ages six, three, and one. They need a mother who is fully present, happy, and relaxed. I do not have the energy and spirit to raise four young children. The option of abortion enters my mind. The thought horrifies me, but I feel backed into a corner.

My physician tells me that if I carry on with the pregnancy I will have to discontinue one of my medications. It has taken me years of gradually increasing doses of this medicine to overcome an allergy to it, and, so far, it has saved me from major surgery.

My husband worries about my getting very sick and not being there for him or the children. He has visions of himself as a single father of four children. Thinking over the state of my health, he feels sure that I need to end this pregnancy.

December 25, 1990—At Midnight Mass I pray as fervently as I can. I know that if anything can convert me, this magical liturgy, the celebration of the unlikely infant, should do it. Could we make room in our crowded lives, could I make room in my diseased and aging body for this infant?

Being Catholic, I feel alienated from my church when I most need it. At a time when I am very vulnerable, I cannot take the risk of seeking help from anyone who would condemn me simply for considering abortion or who might not keep my experience confidential. So I avoid any counselor with a pro-life bias. With the help of a women's health center, I find a counselor who will express no point of view. But the counseling seems superficial. Since I am obviously not happy to be pregnant, she concludes—too easily—that I must want an abortion.

I take my plight directly to God through prayer. I receive the answer that, having borne three children already, I know the gift of a baby. But I can give back the gift if the burden is too great, and it will be taken back into the universe. The greatest punishment I will receive is that which I am already suffering—the knowledge that I will never know this child.

This child, already built to outlast me, will never see the light of day, never be loved by its sisters and brother, will never learn or marry or have children, never grow old.

Making the Appointment

My husband makes an appointment for me at a "women's clinic" in a large city a hundred miles away. I tell the counselor there that I will only terminate this pregnancy if I can do it very early, before the baby takes form, before there is a heartbeat. But I am informed that they will not do abortions before eight weeks of pregnancy; otherwise it cannot be done properly.

I am in the most hellish situation I can imagine. I carry the pregnancy for three weeks more so the embryo can grow large enough to be destroyed.

During those weeks I develop an odd relationship with this incipient baby. Even though an abortion is scheduled, I cannot

167

imagine drinking alcohol during Christmas and New Year's festivities while I am pregnant.

January 7, 1991—My child's last night. I cry as I try to drift off to sleep. I say good-bye to the little creature and tell the child I love it. I dream that I go out to a field and release the being. I see it flutter out of me and into the sky like a butterfly.

January 8, 1991—It's a cold, dark, two-hour ride before dawn to the clinic. I remember last night's dream, which was my true good-bye. Now I steel myself for hard reality. No butterflies and meadows now. This being will be vacuumed through a tube and put out with the trash. . . .

Depression

Back at home, I sleep well for the first time in several weeks. Then I fall into a period of despair. I stop seeing friends. I have told none of them what I've done and now feel that I live in a different universe from those good mothers. I have a few really bad nights where I consider, with enough vividness to frighten me, the idea of jumping off a bridge into the river.

When I am not in despair, I feel nothing. The easy eradication of an incipient person makes my own life, as well as my children's, seem fragile and meaningless. We could so easily not be here, have never existed. One piece of the mind of God has evaporated and become lost in the universe.

August 19, 1991—My due date. I have a private burial ceremony in the back yard for the child whose name is known by no one but me. Under a lilac bush I bury the only concrete evidence that this being existed—the blue-tipped plastic stick, indicating a positive result, from my home pregnancy test. I lay a withered carnation on the ground.

I know that I have passed by any greatness of spirit. Had I been Mary, Jesus would never have been born.

I remain depressed through autumn and winter. . . .

The Healing Begins

July 1992—I contact a minister of the United Church of Christ, whose name was given to me by Project Rachel [a post-abortion counseling program]. She invites me to her home on a sunny summer afternoon. There, over coffee at her dining room table, she listens to my story. I cry lots, telling her that I don't know how I'll get beyond the pain. She brings me a box of Kleenex and recounts the story of Jacob, how he wrestled with the angel and received his new name, Israel, but walked with a limp the rest of his life.

She tells me I am not alone, that she had counseled a militant prolifer who, when her own teenage daughter became pregnant, obtained an abortion for her.

Though I am grateful for this accepting woman, this minister who shares coffee and Kleenex, I remain troubled by the fact that I am actually excommunicated from the church. According to church law, I am digging myself in a continually deeper hole toward hell by continuing to participate in the Eucharist. But without God, without my community, I would die spiritually.

I think of the many Catholic women like me who must be suffering alone and cannot summon the courage to reconcile within the church.

Forgiveness

Autumn 1992—My family and I spend this season living in a college community far from home, in the countryside. In this pastoral setting, in this leave of absence from home and routine, strong bonds are forged among our group of new friends. My depression begins to lift. I realize I am smiling and laughing more than I have in years.

I walk miles each day. One sunny afternoon on a country walk under the wide October sky, I can palpably feel redemption.

Two months later, at the end of my last day at that place, as the red sun touches the winter landscape like an eye shutting peacefully on a season of grace, I feel God's hand touch the top of my head.

A Heavy Price

The denial of the biological facts and the violent subversion of the natural process of pregnancy by abortion must come with a heavy price: a dead child, a victimized mother, a hurt family, and a disordered society. . . .

The plain truth is that a woman submitting to a voluntary abortion has agreed to the killing of her child. The abortion denies not only the social role of women as supportive, loving, life-giving, and maternal; it also denies the entire biological reality of a woman who is designed precisely to care for and nurture the child in her womb. Such a willful breach with a woman's natural role is bound to have severe repercussions.

Wanda Franz, *National Right to Life News*, April 14, 1993.

I return home knowing that God forgave me long ago. I begin to forgive myself. But I crave the kind of reconciliation that we as flesh and blood creatures most understand, to be touched and forgiven by another human being. That is what I need to be set free.

I have begun talking to a counselor. She happens to be an active Catholic, but she does not know of any priest in my city whom she would trust to listen to me with compassion. If, indeed, there are Catholic clergy who are approachable, they are well hidden.

I do not ask the church to change its position on abortion. I am not trying to justify my action or exonerate myself. But I do ask the church for a more open invitation to counseling and reconciliation, as well as reassurance to women that they will not be shamed or condemned. Had I not feared harsh judgment, I might have sought a counselor who might have helped me to see how I could bear this baby.

I also ask for understanding. My choice was not simple: it was not made out of disregard for life but because of the desire to protect my family. No one loved that incipient child more than I did.

I ask for the type of compassion and friendship that Jesus offered Mary Magdalene.

> "The allegation that legal abortions, performed under safe medical conditions, cause severe and lasting psychological damage is not borne out by the facts."

Post-Abortion Syndrome Is a Myth

Nada L. Stotland

Nada L. Stotland is an associate professor of psychiatry and obstetrics and gynecology at the University of Chicago.
In the following viewpoint, Stotland argues that there is no factual basis behind the allegation that women suffer lasting psychological trauma after an abortion. Women are hospitalized for psychiatric reasons more frequently after childbirth than after an abortion, she maintains. Most women feel relief after an abortion, Stotland asserts, and the few women who say they are depressed after an abortion are usually experiencing feelings of sadness rather than the psychiatric disorder of depression.

As you read, consider the following questions:

1. As cited by Stotland, what conclusion did C. Everett Koop reach after interviewing abortion experts about abortion's effects on women?
2. What circumstances may increase a woman's feeling of distress about her abortion, according to the author?
3. What should be the goal of society and medicine concerning unwanted pregnancies, in Stotland's opinion?

From Nada L. Stotland, "The Myth of the Abortion Trauma Syndrome," *JAMA*, October 21, 1992. Copyright ©1992 by the American Medical Association. Reprinted with permission.

This is a viewpoint about a medical syndrome that does not exist. A so-called abortion trauma syndrome has been described in written material and on television and radio programs. For example, leaflets warning of deleterious physical and emotional consequences of abortion have been distributed on the streets of cities in the United States. Women who have undergone induced abortion are said to suffer an "abortion trauma syndrome" or "postabortion trauma" that will cause long-term damage to their health. One such leaflet states,

> Most often a woman will feel the consequences of her decision within days of her abortion. If they don't appear immediately, they will appear as she gets older. Emotional scars include unexplained depression, a loss of the ability to get close to others, repressed emotions, a hardening of the spirit, thwarted maternal instincts (which may lead to child abuse or neglect later in life), intense feelings of guilt and thoughts of suicide. Don't be fooled—every abortion leaves emotional scars.

Press reports indicate that women who seek care and counseling at so-called pregnancy crisis clinics are verbally presented with similar statements.

Syndrome and Trauma

"Syndrome" indicates a constellation of signs and symptoms recognized by the medical community as characterizing a disease or abnormal condition. "Trauma" is borrowed from "posttraumatic stress disorder," a psychiatric syndrome defined in the *Diagnostic and Statistical Manual of Mental Disorders* as a disabling condition characterized by nightmares and flashbacks, precipitated by a traumatic event outside the range of usual human experience. News reporters from all sections of the United States have requested information about abortion trauma syndrome from the American Psychiatric Association. Unfortunately, it is impossible to document the sources of the allegations that concern these journalists because they are often not traceable through the media or found in the scientific literature. It is to bring the discussion into the scientific medical literature that this contribution has been written.

Abortion is a subject that is embroiled in fierce debate. The U.S. Supreme Court's increasingly permissive stance toward individual states' restricting abortion has precipitated divisive arguments among individuals, social groups, jurists, and legislators. The same is true of a 1991 federal regulation forbidding some health care providers to discuss abortion at federally funded clinics. The heat of the conflict tends to melt boundaries between medicine and philosophy, between church and state, between demonstrated fact and personal belief. The legislative and judicial outcome of this debate may profoundly affect both the physical and psychological health of the population as well as the practice of medicine.

Our patients look to us, their physicians, to provide sound scientific information to help them make informed decisions about health issues. The allegation that legal abortions, performed under safe medical conditions, cause severe and lasting psychological damage is not borne out by the facts. Prior to the 1973 *Roe v Wade* decision of the Supreme Court, valid scientific investigation of the sequelae of abortion was precluded by the criminal and illicit nature of the procedure. It was also impossible to distinguish the effects of the procedure from those of the frightening and often dangerous circumstances under which it was performed. While he was Surgeon General of the United States, C. Everett Koop, MD, interviewed representatives from a wide range of groups favoring, opposing, and expert about access to abortion, in the course of researching a report on abortion's effects on women that had been requested by then President Ronald Reagan. After hearing and reviewing the evidence, Dr. Koop wrote President Reagan to state that the available scientific evidence did not demonstrate significant negative (or positive) mental health effects of abortion.

A critical examination of the psychiatric impact of abortion requires the consideration of underlying realities and a summary of the relevant scientific literature.

Underlying Realities

An uninterrupted pregnancy eventuates in labor and delivery. Therefore, any physical and psychological sequelae of legal abortion can only be meaningfully understood in contrast with those of illegal abortion or unwanted childbirth. After undesired childbirth, a woman must face either the stresses of relinquishing a child for adoption or those of rearing a child.

Abortion is a consideration for women who become pregnant under problematic circumstances, in which they feel that the birth of a child might be untenable. Such circumstances commonly include the threat or reality of abandonment by the woman's male partner or the absence of an ongoing relationship with him, financial deprivation, lack of social support, the need to care for other young children, the possible loss of educational and career opportunities, the diagnosis of fetal defect, and/or an impregnation by rape or incest. A birth control method may have failed; the woman may be unwilling or unable to care for a child. She may be physically or mentally ill or disabled. She may have suffered physical or psychiatric complications after childbirth in the past. All of these circumstances may influence subsequent psychiatric reactions regardless of the woman's decision to abort or to continue the pregnancy.

The outcome of any medical procedure is demonstrably shaped by the general and individual social and psychological climate in which it is performed. Criminalization and/or membership in a religious or social group opposed to abortion can be expected to increase a woman's feeling of distress, as can insensitive, negative, or hostile behavior and remarks by health care professionals or others she encounters in the process of considering or obtaining an abortion. S. Meikle et al. studied 100 women applying for abortions before and after abortion was legalized and noted a comparative decrease in the incidence of emotional distress related to the increased social acceptance of the procedure.

Mentally Healthier Women

My experiences as a family physician over the past 20 years certainly confirm Nada L. Stotland's conclusion that this [post-abortion] syndrome does not exist. . . . My impression from following many women [with unwanted pregnancies] is that those who chose to terminate the pregnancy, in general, had better long-term psychological adjustment than those who elected to continue the pregnancy.

Robert L. Blake, *Journal of the American Medical Association*, May 5, 1993.

Abortion is a reality, practiced throughout history, in every area of the world, regardless of religious and cultural belief and whether legal or outlawed. In 1972, the year before the *Roe v Wade* decision, approximately 1 million illegal abortions were performed in the United States alone.

Data in the Literature

An extensive search of MEDLINE, Psychological Information Data Base, Sociological Abstracts, Health Information Data Base, and review articles and their bibliographies reveals that there is no specific abortion trauma syndrome described—in survey populations or as individual cases—in the psychiatric and psychological literature. A small number of papers and books based on anecdotal evidence and stressing negative effects have been presented and published under religious auspices and in the nonspecialty literature.

Significant psychiatric sequelae after abortion are rare, as documented in numerous methodologically sound prospective studies in the United States and in European countries. Comprehensive reviews of this literature have recently been performed and confirm this conclusion. The incidence of diagnosed psychiatric illness and hospitalization is considerably lower following abortion than following childbirth. In one large prospective British population study, psychosis occurred after delivery in an average of 1.7 cases per 1000 and after abortion in 0.3 of 1000.

Significant psychiatric illness following abortion occurs most commonly in women who were psychiatrically ill before pregnancy, in those who decided to undergo abortion under external pressure, and in those who underwent abortion in aversive circumstances, for example, abandonment. B. Lask attributed the adverse reactions in 11% of the subjects he studied to those factors.

The term "unwanted pregnancy" indicates that the woman regrets the fact that conception occurred. Abortion, whether spontaneous or induced, entails loss. Both regret and loss result in sadness. The word "depression," which is both a common term for a feeling of sadness and the technical term for a psychiatric disorder, can be especially confusing. A symptom or a feeling is not equivalent to a disease. Some women who undergo abortion experience transient feelings of stress and sadness, as distinguished from psychiatric illness, before and for a short time afterward. The majority experience relief after the procedure. Henry Steven Greer et al. interviewed 360 women before they underwent abortions and at follow-up an average of 18 months later. The subjects demonstrated significant improvement in guilt feelings, personal relationships, and psychiatric symptoms. Of 207 women followed by J. Partridge et al., 94% reported that their mental health improved or remained the same after abortion. Many women report that the difficult decision to terminate a pregnancy was a maturational point in their lives, one at which they experienced taking charge of their futures for the first time. A 1992 study of a national sample of over 5000 U.S. women followed for 8 years concluded that the experience of abortion did not have an independent relationship to women's well-being, and that there was no evidence of widespread postabortion trauma.

Abortion is a weighty issue and a medical procedure about which both physicians and the lay public have a wide variety of profound feelings and views. In their professional roles, physicians counsel, advocate for, and treat individual patients on the basis of medical knowledge and in the patient's best interest. It would be preferable to use the resources of society and medicine to prevent unwanted pregnancies and to decrease the ensuing demand for abortions, but it is unlikely that the demand will ever be eliminated. Therefore, physicians must provide patients with accurate information about abortion's medical and psychological implications. Scientific studies indicate that legal abortion results in fewer deleterious sequelae for women compared with other possible outcomes of unwanted pregnancy. There is no evidence of an abortion trauma syndrome.

Periodical Bibliography

The following articles have been selected to supplement the diverse views presented in this chapter. Addresses are provided for periodicals not indexed in the *Readers' Guide to Periodical Literature*, the *Alternative Press Index*, or the *Social Sciences Index*.

Marion Asnes — "RU-486: What You Don't Know," *Working Woman*, November 1994.

Sharon Begley — "Abortion by Prescription," *Newsweek*, September 11, 1995.

Janet R. Daling et al. — "Risk of Breast Cancer Among Young Women: Relationship to Induced Abortion," *Journal of the National Cancer Institute*, November 2, 1994. Available from 9030 Old Georgetown Rd., Bethesda, MD 20814.

Christine Gorman — "Do Abortions Raise the Risk of Breast Cancer?" *Time*, November 7, 1994.

Gayle M.B. Hanson — "'Morning After' Pill Has Political Side Effects," *Insight*, July 4, 1994. Available from 3600 New York Ave. NE, Washington, DC 20002.

M. Klitsch — "Abortion Experience Does Not Appear to Reduce Women's Self-Esteem or Psychological Well-Being," *Family Planning Perspectives*, November/December 1992. Available from 120 Wall St., New York, NY 10005.

Polly A. Newcomb et al. — "Pregnancy Termination in Relation to Risk of Breast Cancer," *JAMA*, January 24–31, 1996. Available from Subscriber Services, American Medical Association, 515 N. State St., Chicago, IL 60610.

Debra Rosenberg, Michele Ingrassia, and Sharon Begley — "Blood and Tears," *Newsweek*, September 18, 1995.

Lynn Rosenberg — "Induced Abortion and Breast Cancer: More Scientific Data Are Needed," *Journal of the National Cancer Institute*, November 2, 1994.

Jo Ann Rosenfeld and Tom Townsend — "Doesn't Everyone Grieve in the Abortion Choice?" *Journal of Clinical Ethics*, Summer 1993. Available from 107 E. Church St., Frederick, MD 21701.

Andrea Sachs — "Abortion Pills on Trial," *Time*, December 5, 1994.

Is Research Using Aborted Fetal Tissue Ethical?

Abortion

Chapter Preface

Fetal tissue is uniquely suitable for medical research and transplantation. It is nonspecific, meaning that it has the potential to develop into any kind of tissue—muscle or organ, for example—if it is transplanted into humans. When used to treat diseases, fetal tissue takes over the function of damaged tissue. This finding has encouraged millions of people with conditions such as juvenile diabetes, epilepsy, muscular dystrophy, Alzheimer's, Parkinson's, and immunological diseases to hope for an effective treatment or cure in the near future.

Yet in March 1988 fetal tissue research was temporarily banned until a panel of experts had issued its recommendations on the ethical, legal, and medical aspects of the research to the National Institutes of Health (NIH) and the Department of Health and Human Services (HHS). The 21-member panel consisted of nine scientists, three abortion opponents, one citizen's representative, and a number of attorneys and bioethicists. Supporters of the ban argued that government funding of fetal tissue research would encourage abortion. Many women would be swayed toward having the procedure, they maintained, because of the possibility that the aborted fetus would be used to benefit humanity. Opponents of the ban cited studies in which women claimed that fetal tissue research would have little effect on their decision to have an abortion.

After meeting three times and hearing over fifty witnesses, the panel endorsed fetal tissue research provided that the government regulate and monitor the process. The strict ethical guidelines recommended by the panel were similar to those of other countries that allow fetal tissue research. The panel concluded that although abortion is morally relevant to the issue, fetal tissue research is "acceptable public policy" because of the "possibility of relieving suffering and saving life."

Despite the panel's recommendation, HHS secretary Louis Sullivan directed that the temporary ban be made permanent. Allowing researchers to use tissue from aborted fetuses would "increase the incidence of abortion across the country," he maintained. In 1992, George Bush vetoed an attempt by Congress to lift the transplant ban in order to "prevent taxpayer funds from being used for research that many Americans find morally repugnant and because of its potential for promoting and legitimizing abortion."

The ban remained in effect until January 1993 when Bill Clinton restored federal funding of fetal tissue research and transplants. Despite the lifting of the funding ban, the controversy over the ethics of fetal tissue research continues. The following chapter examines some of the debates over this issue.

"No reason could ever be good enough to rationalize the possible abuses of . . . fetuses to prolong the health and life of another."

Fetal Tissue Research Is Unethical

Mary DeTurris

Using the tissue of aborted fetuses for medical purposes is unethical, argues Mary DeTurris in the following viewpoint. Fetal tissue research, she contends, will make society dependent on abortion to provide a constant supply of fetal tissue. DeTurris maintains that once society accepts using aborted fetal tissue for the treatment of serious diseases, it will eventually become acceptable to use aborted fetal tissue for nonessential medical procedures. DeTurris is the former managing editor of the weekly newspaper *Catholic New York*.

As you read, consider the following questions:

1. Why might the use of fetal tissue for medical research lead to abortion becoming an industry, according to DeTurris?
2. In the author's opinion, how does the Parkinson's disease research resemble a medieval experiment?
3. What purposes might fetal tissue be used for if fetal tissue transplants become the norm, according to Bernard Nathanson, as cited by DeTurris?

Mary DeTurris, "Let's Put a Limit on Fetal-Tissue Research," *U.S. Catholic*, October 1994. Reprinted with permission.

Fetal-tissue research. The words sound antiseptic enough, almost vague. How bad could it be? Science must have its reasons. Right? Unfortunately science does have its reasons, but none of them is good enough to justify what will amount to the harvesting of body parts now that electively aborted fetal tissue can be used for transplants. No reason could ever be good enough to rationalize the possible abuses of pregnant women or fetuses to prolong the health and life of another. And yet, that is what this type of fetal-tissue research is all about—at its best.

Eugenics Gone Mad

At its worst, it is a Nazi-like effort to create a perfect human race, where diseases are "cured" by taking the healthy cells and organs of a developing baby and transplanting them into a sick person. Fetal-tissue research is nothing new, although it sounds like something out of a science-fiction story. And it is not likely to stop with cures for diseases. This is a slippery slope of the most dangerous kind, and at the bottom is eugenics gone mad.

As far back as 1928, there have been attempts to transplant fetal tissue, which is especially suitable for such operations because it is immature and flexible. According to physician Bernard Nathanson, who once ran one of the largest abortion clinics in the world and is now an avid prolife activist, fetal tissue is desirable because it can flourish even in an aging recipient; its proximity to diseased cells helps them regenerate; it matures and functions as healthy adult cells would; and it is not likely to be destroyed by the adult immune system.

In recent years, research has focused on the diseases most likely to be cured with fetal-tissue transplants: Parkinson's, diabetes, and Alzheimer's. For many people battling these chronic and often debilitating illnesses—and for the loved ones who must watch them suffer—these experiments may seem like a miracle cure, the answer to a prayer. And that's understandable in many ways. I have family members and friends who have diabetes and Parkinson's. When I try to put myself in their position, it's easy to see why good, moral people would opt for fetal-tissue treatment. After all, the fetuses used for the operations are voluntarily aborted; they were going to die anyway. At least through transplants their lives take on some meaning.

If one of these operations could save a parent, a spouse, a child, wouldn't it be easy to justify using tissue from a baby who was never going to be born? Wouldn't it be better to save one life rather than lose two? It's hard for an outsider to make that call when another's life hangs in the balance. Parkinson's disease alone afflicts more than half-a-million Americans, and although medicine can control the symptoms at first, its effectiveness wears off after time. Is it up to us to say that those people should live a life of misery even when the very tissue that could save them will be thrown out with medical waste at clinics across the country?

Trading One Life for Another

Maybe it's not politically correct, but I would have to say, yes, it is up to U.S. citizens. No matter how bad the illness, we must look beyond the less-than-descriptive words of medical technology and admit what lies at the heart of fetal-tissue research on electively aborted fetuses: trading one life for another. With the number of patients who would want this tissue, it would be impossible for even the high abortion rate in this country to keep up with the demand. So there is the danger that this will become an industry.

The protest will probably not begin any time soon, especially since President Clinton, in one of his first official acts as president, rescinded a five-year ban on using fetal tissue from elective abortions for transplants. Obviously, the government and special advisory boards established to research this issue have not always felt justified in supporting such procedures. This ban was established in 1989 after the Department of Health and Human Services reached a decision that there existed a very viable and real threat that the incidence of abortion would increase across the country. Those justifying the federal ban feared that if large amounts of fetal tissue were required for transplants, society may for the first time need and depend on the practice of elective abortion, rather than merely tolerate it.

Not only has the ban been lifted, but in 1994 federal money—to the tune of $4.5 million—was awarded by the National Institute of Neurological Disorders and Stroke to three hospitals for the sole purpose of transplanting fetal tissue into Parkinson's patients. It is believed that the tissue will assist Parkinson's sufferers in the production of dopamine, a brain chemical that is deficient in these patients. Previously such experiments were privately funded.

Medieval Experiments

Columbia-Presbyterian Medical Center in New York City; North Shore University Hospital in Manhasset, New York; and the University of Colorado Health Sciences Center in Denver will share the grant money for the experiments on 40 Parkinson's patients. Twenty will receive injections of fetal tissue into their brains; another 20 will receive placebo injections, although they will have to go through the grueling operation that requires having two holes drilled into the skull while awake. Neither the patients nor the doctors will know who received the fake injections.

First of all, drilling holes into people's skulls as part of a random experiment seems a bit medieval to me. Couple that with the fact that many scientists admit that these transplant operations have not proven to be all that effective and should be further tested on animals and you have a very questionable—ethically, morally, and medically—experiment before you even begin to address the gruesome task of taking fetal tissue.

In addition to the physical brutality of removing fetal tissue, there are broader concerns as well. For instance, the demand for fetal tissue would far outweigh the supply, especially since each patient would require tissue from several unborn babies and because many methods of abortion would not preserve the tissue as required or retrieve it at the appropriate stage of development.

Good Cannot Redeem Evil

Taking innocent human lives in order to save other human lives undermines a basic principle of the moral code that sustains our society and the legal code that regulates our common life. . . .

Fetal tissue is human tissue—not even *Roe v. Wade* denies that. This tissue was once part of a developing life that has been destroyed and dispatched. Harvesting that tissue in order to save or sustain another, wanted human life cannot redeem the taking of life in the first place (drawing good out of evil). For that reason after World War II the scientific community chose to forego whatever knowledge might derive from Nazi medical experiments.

Commonweal, June 19, 1992.

Some have suggested that this will lead to the cultivation of fetuses strictly for transplant parts, and it's easy to see why. Others have said that it will create a huge black market, with the women of the Third World becoming likely targets. Women in crisis pregnancies might be persuaded that their abortions would save the lives of others, and thereby make abortion a selfless, almost noble choice.

Instead of spending all this money and effort on morally questionable methods of disease control, scientists should focus their work on finding true cures that don't come at such a high price.

But cures and transplants are only the tip of the iceberg in the use of tissue of electively aborted fetuses. Gruesome cannot even begin to describe some of the other "research" with regard to the unborn. A British scientist made the news recently when he announced that he and his peers at Edinburgh University in Scotland had performed experiments on mice that gave them hope that some day, although it's not being done now, it will be possible to implant eggs from aborted babies into sterile women. In other words, they hope to produce children whose mothers were never born. Imagine the problems that would plague such children, not to mention the myriad moral and ethical questions that society would have to face.

I suppose some of this sounds almost too hard to believe. Maybe we can convince ourselves that it will never happen, that society and the government won't let it. But it is happening, just as test-tube babies and surrogate mothers went from being the stuff of make-believe to the stuff of everyday life, complete with courtroom dramas and made-for-TV movies.

Sliding Down the Slippery Slope

But this is not television, and it's not make-believe. And who's to say it will stop there? What's to keep doctors from taking parts from not-so-healthy newborns to help those who have a better chance of survival or from taking organs from an elderly patient to prolong the life of a middle-aged patient? The possibilities are endless, and unless we start paying closer attention to the actions behind the technical language, there is no telling what—or who—will be next.

Bernard Nathanson, a visiting fellow at the Kennedy Institute of Ethics at Georgetown University in Washington, D.C., has suggested that if ovary and brain cell transplants become the norm, then widespread use of the tissue of electively aborted fetuses for cosmetic surgery, such as skin and hair transplants, won't be far behind.

It is up to each one of us to help stop the slide down the slippery slope. Then again, maybe the slippery slope isn't really an accurate description anymore. Perhaps, instead, we are peering over the edge of an abyss, where life has no value and birth is something relegated to petri dishes and laboratories. It's time to take a step back before we go over the brink and can't see right from wrong.

"*Whatever wrong might be involved in use of fetal tissue obtained from induced abortions is outweighed by the potential benefits to patients.*"

Fetal Tissue Research Is Ethical

Carson Strong

In the following viewpoint, Carson Strong argues that using aborted fetal tissue in medical research and treatments is ethical because the procedures' benefits outweigh any wrong incurred by the abortion. In addition, he contends, the fetus has no individual rights that can be violated. The unethical use of abortion for medical research can be prevented by establishing strict guidelines, he maintains. Strong is an associate professor in the Department of Human Values and Ethics at the University of Tennessee's College of Medicine in Memphis.

As you read, consider the following questions:

1. According to Strong, what are some of the diseases that might be treated with fetal tissue transplants?
2. Why is fetal tissue from spontaneous abortion unsatisfactory for use in research or transplants, according to Strong?
3. Why are fetal tissue transplants beneficial to medical science even if the treatments are found to be ineffective, in the author's opinion?

Reprinted from Carson Strong, "Fetal Tissue Transplantation: Can It Be Morally Insulated from Abortion?" *Journal of Medical Ethics* 17: 70-76 (June 1991). Reprinted by permission of the publisher, BMJ Publishing Group, London.

In recent years, transplantation of fetal tissue has emerged as a possible approach to the treatment of a variety of human diseases. One area of research that seems promising involves the treatment of Parkinson's disease. . . .

Another area of research involves treatment of diabetes mellitus. Transplantation of fetal pancreatic tissue has reversed drug-induced diabetes in mice and rats. Initial clinical studies have shown that human fetal pancreatic tissue survives in the human host. Fetal tissue also has been transplanted in the treatment of DiGeorge's syndrome, aplastic anaemia, leukaemia and severe combined immunodeficiency. Other conditions that animal research suggests might be treatable by fetal tissue transplantation include Alzheimer's disease, Huntington's disease, spinal cord injury, and neuroendocrine deficiencies. . . .

The Ethical Controversy

The ethics of fetal tissue transplantation was debated by the National Institutes of Health (NIH) Human Fetal Tissue Transplantation Research Panel. The panel was established in 1988 after the Assistant Secretary for Health issued a moratorium on funding of research using fetal tissue. [The moratorium was lifted by Bill Clinton in January 1993.] The charge to the panel was to examine the ethical issues and advise NIH on whether such research should be supported by government funds.

Ethical controversy has arisen because the source of fetal tissue is induced abortions. Tissue from spontaneous abortions is generally considered unsatisfactory because of the high rate of fetal pathology, such as chromosomal abnormalities and viral infections, as well as anoxia [an abnormally low amount of oxygen in the body tissues] due to the delay between death of the fetus and expulsion from the uterus. Opposition to use of fetal tissue is based on the view that abortion is wrong and that tissue use is tied to the morality of abortion. . . .

If [fetal] tissue use is ethical, then it is important to state explicitly why it is so. One must argue either that there is nothing morally problematic about abortion, *or* that whatever wrong is involved in using tissue from induced abortions is morally *outweighed* by other considerations.

It is not plausible to maintain that there is nothing morally problematic about abortion. At the very least, one can argue that the potential of the fetus to become a person gives abortion *some* moral significance. However, it can be argued that whatever wrong might be involved in use of fetal tissue obtained from induced abortions is outweighed by the potential benefits to patients. This moral balancing involves two basic factors: the degree of wrongness in using the tissue; and the degree and likelihood of potential benefits to patients resulting from tissue use. The less the wrongness and the greater and more likely the benefits, the stronger is the argument that fetal tissue transplantation is ethically justifiable.

No Moral Interests

Several considerations suggest that the degree of wrongness is relatively low. First, it can be argued that fetuses in early gestation are not persons. One such argument is based on the implausibility of holding that they are the type of individuals that can have rights. It has been persuasively argued that a prerequisite of having rights is that one be a type of individual that can have moral interests. Moreover, it is not reasonable to think that individuals lacking desires, cognitive awareness, and perceptions have interests. With regard to *substantia nigra* [a section of the brain] transplants, tissue would be obtained from fetuses at approximately 8–11 weeks gestational age. Although the stage of gestation at which fetal perception begins is not clear, current research suggests that it is considerably later than the 8–11 week period. The brain structures that give rise to such experiences are not sufficiently developed until later. For example, thalamocortical connections necessary for pain perception do not seem to be established until some time between 20 and 24 weeks of gestation. For these reasons, the claim that fetuses at 8–11 weeks gestational age have rights is questionable. And if they do not have rights, then they cannot be persons, because part of what it means to say that one is a person is that one has a right to life.

Fetal Rights

It might be objected that interests the fetus will have in the future can create rights that the fetus possesses now. On this basis one might claim, for example, that the fetus has a right not to be subjected to high-risk, non-therapeutic research because at some future time the fetus will have an interest in being free of harms that might occur through such research. Even if we were to accept this objection, however, it would not follow that the fetus now has a right to life. If the fetus now is killed, there will be no future individual having interests. Because an individual with interests never exists, it is difficult to claim that a right to life— or any right, for that matter—is violated by killing the fetus.

Second, a lack of personhood status of the fetuses in question has implications for the argument concerning informed consent. If these fetuses are not persons, then it is doubtful that respectful treatment of the fetal remains involves exactly the same requirements as respectful treatment of adult cadavers. Specifically, although consent for use of adult cadavers is necessary, it is not clear that it is needed for respectful use of fetal tissue early in gestation. Consent for use of fetal tissue seems to be required, rather, in order to protect the interests of the woman having the abortion. Third, a lack of personhood status has implications for the argument that the number of abortions will increase. If fetuses early in gestation lack rights and interests, then an increase in abortions does not have the same degree of moral significance that it would have if fetuses had rights and interests that needed protection. These considerations do not imply that there is *nothing at all* morally problematic about use of tissue from induced abortions. If human fetuses in early gestation have *some* degree of moral standing, then an increase in abortions would seem to be morally undesirable to some degree. However, the above considerations suggest that the wrongness of using early-gestation fetal tissue is not . . . great. . . .

Fetal Tissue Transplants
Do Not Affect Abortion Decisions

In a random survey of female patients at a Toronto hospital, 266 women were asked:

If you became pregnant and knew that tissue from the fetus could be used to help someone suffering from Parkinson's disease, would you be more likely to have an abortion?

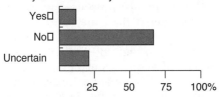

If you became pregnant and knew that tissue from the fetus could be used to help someone suffering from Parkinson's disease, how would you feel about having an abortion?

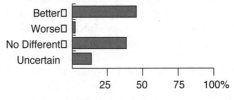

Douglas K. Martin et al., *Canadian Medical Association Journal*, September 1, 1995.

Moreover, it can be argued that the potential for benefit from fetal tissue transplantation is morally significant. Those who might benefit—sufferers of Parkinson's disease, diabetes, and other disabling disorders—are indeed persons, a fact that is absolutely without controversy. Thus, if there is benefit to those individuals, it will undoubtedly have moral significance because it is a benefit to persons. Moreover, there is a reasonable chance that there will be at least some benefit from going forward with this area of clinical research. Even if it turns out that fetal tissue transplantation does not provide effective treatments, knowledge will be gained about the human body, disease, and therapeutic interventions. Such knowledge often has a way of eventually contributing, in greater or less degree, to the development of useful applications. In addition, if therapies prove effective, the degree of the benefits might be great.

In summary, transplantation and research involving human fetal tissue appear ethically justifiable because the degree of wrongness that might be involved seems relatively low, no rights would be violated (assuming the woman having the abortion gives informed consent to use of the fetal tissue, and other pertinent guidelines and laws are followed), at least some benefit is reasonably expected, and great benefits are possible. . . .

Moral Considerations

In order to defend a view concerning the ethics of fetal tissue transplantation, it seems necessary to take a position concerning the moral status of early-gestation fetuses, as is done in the above argument. Moreover, the above approach helps explain why it is appropriate to adopt guidelines that provide greater insulation between research and abortions. It is not desirable to increase the number of abortions or to use tissue in a manner that some find offensive. Such features of fetal tissue use can be countenanced only if they are outweighed by other moral considerations. Other things being equal, it is morally preferable to minimise these effects. The greater the insulation produced by guidelines, the less pronounced will be any increase in the number of abortions. Moreover, the health interests of the woman having an abortion are protected by insulating procedures such as not allowing the timing or method of abortion to be influenced by the research uses of the tissue. In addition, there is a consensus that certain activities should be flatly proscribed, such as abortions for the sole purpose of obtaining the tissue. This makes it appropriate to have additional insulating guidelines, such as a rule that the woman having the abortion may not designate the recipient of the tissue. Appropriate insulating guidelines have been recommended by several committees in addition to the NIH panel.

It might be objected that the above argument is utilitarian, that it approves the wronging of fetuses in order to produce a net benefit overall. However, this objection fails to consider that an essential feature of the argument is that no rights would be violated, provided that relevant guidelines and laws are followed. The potential benefits of fetal tissue transplantation are a compelling consideration only because it is reasonable to think that the research can be performed without violating rights. To appeal to benefits in situations in which no rights are violated does not make one a utilitarian.

"No real good can come from the murder of unborn babies."

Using Aborted Fetal Ovary Tissue Is Unethical

Lawrence F. Roberge

In the following viewpoint, Lawrence F. Roberge takes issue with a proposed procedure in which egg cells from the ovaries of aborted fetuses would be transplanted into sterile women. Using egg cells from aborted fetuses to help infertile women become pregnant is unethical and wrong, he contends. The many legal and moral questions concerning the status of children born from this type of procedure exemplify why this research should be prohibited, he maintains. Roberge is a bioethicist, an adjunct professor of biology at Bay Bath College in Longmeadow, Massachusetts, and the author of *The Cost of Abortion*.

As you read, consider the following questions:

1. Why is fetal tissue useful in transplant operations, according to Roberge?
2. In what three ways does Roger Gosden propose using aborted fetal tissue, as cited by Roberge?
3. According to the author, what are the limitations to fetal tissue transplantation?

Lawrence Roberge, "Transplantation of Aborted Fetal Ova: A Short Analysis," *Wanderer*, August 4, 1994. Reprinted with permission.

Another aborted fetal tissue transplant experiment hit the front page of the newspapers across the globe in 1994. These transplants will not save the life of the recipient, but merely restore fertility.

Transplanting Aborted Fetal Tissue

Dr. Roger Gosden of Edinburgh University has requested permission to use aborted human fetal ovarian tissue to restore the fertility of sterile women. The technique involves taking ovarian tissue from aborted fetuses (babies) and extracting the ova (egg cells). The ova would be cultured to maturity, fertilized by in vitro methods, and then implanted into the recipient mother. Britain's 21-member Human Fertilization and Embryology Authority is considering his request. If granted, experts believe that the technique could be perfected by 1997.

But *why* fetal tissue? Why "harvest" tissue from aborted babies? Fetal tissue research has attracted much attention in the scientific community since the 1980s. It has been found that fetal tissue is useful because it is less likely to be rejected by the recipient; it usually will develop cellular connections with the surrounding blood and neural networks (especially important for neural tissue transplants); and it is targeted to treat very difficult diseases like diabetes, Parkinson's, blindness, and Alzheimer's.

A paper written by Dr. Gosden in the April 1992 *Journal of Assisted Reproduction and Genetics* reviews the outline of this research (i.e., how and why it will work for humans!) a full two years before his research proposal became news. This paper bases his proposal on prior work in which Dr. Gosden has extensively performed mouse fetal tissue transplant studies to restore the fertility of sterile mice. These studies included using mice fetal tissue to restore fertility to sterile mice, restore endocrine function to mice without ovaries, and freezing and storing mouse fetal ovarian tissue for later successful implantation.

Dr. Gosden's work promises to harvest egg cells from aborted fetuses at the 12–16 week stage. They would then fertilize the eggs by in vitro methods and implant them into previously sterile women. These are women born with few egg cells in their ovaries or with gonadal dysgenesis (i.e., never developed ovaries, as for example women who have the genetic disorder Turner's syndrome).

Other Uses of Fetal Tissue

Furthermore, Gosden's transplant work included using fetal follicular cells (i.e., cells which produce the ovarian hormones estrogen and progesterone). Transplants of follicular cells would be used to restore the production of estrogen to protect menopausal women from osteoporosis and the increased risk of cardiovascular disease. Furthermore, it would restore the fertility of women who had prematurely undergone menopause, thereby giving them extended years of childbearing.

Finally, Gosden suggests that further culturing of these ova cells could lead to the development of a cell line for toxicology screening tests. These tests would expose the cell culture (i.e., aborted fetal tissue) to chemicals to determine if the chemical induces mutations of cell damage that could lead to cancer or birth defects.

What Is Next?

The real reason for unease [about fetal ovary transplants], I suspect, is that the middle ground on abortion is awfully slippery turf. If you think abortion is a purely private decision, it's hard to sustain any objection to its particulars. Today, we are talking about inseminating eggs from dead fetuses. Tomorrow, we may be talking about conceiving fetuses solely to furnish body parts for people in need. Someday, when it becomes possible to incubate an embryo to maturity in man-made machines, we could have fetus farms devoted to such purposes.

On the other hand, if you are alarmed by these prospects, you are pushed toward acknowledging that a fetus has some rights worthy of protection. Americans have not gotten to that stage yet. But this controversy may force them to consider how abortion rights have altered our ethical outlook and ask whether they like what they see.

Stephen Chapman, *Conservative Chronicle*, January 26, 1994.

The limitations to fetal tissue transplantation include the social and moral objections to using aborted fetuses. Also, obtaining tissue from spontaneously aborted (miscarriage) fetuses is not possible as the tissue is usually worthless or may be diseased (which may have caused the original miscarriage). Several other limitations to fetal tissue transplantation technology include the high tissue loss upon transplantation; that is, 80–90 percent of all transplanted cells die. Also, as clinical abortions are replaced with abortion induced by RU 486, abortifacient vaccines, and other very early stage abortion techniques, the availability of aborted fetuses will dwindle.

The overall moral and ethical conflicts are vast. As this is reducing a fetus (unborn baby) to a spare-parts box for medical science, one wonders if society will reject this technology because of the moral and ethical problems that would arise. Do we continue to harvest tissues from murdered children? Do we prevent abortions to those who create life with the intent of using the fetus for "spare parts"? What would be the legal status of a child born from a biological mother, but having another genetically true mother (the fetus)? In the day when birth mothers are seeking custody of their children from the adoptive parents, what will be the legal status of children from aborted fetuses?

"Genetically Adopted" Children

One further legal point is the following. Remember all the adopted children who grew up and strongly desired to seek out their birth parents? That is, adults who tried legal and other methods to obtain the identity of their true biological parents. Will this technology spawn a generation of "genetically adopted" children who will wonder who their real mothers are? What will these children grow up and feel? Will they wonder and strive to find out (by legal and other means) who the tissue donor (the aborted fetus) was? Will they strive to find their grandmother (the mother of the aborted fetus)? As their "grandmother" will be the one who aborted their "mother," would this aggravate the "grandmother's" post-abortion trauma? Yes, this may sound confusing, *but* consider how confusing it will be for the "children" and the "grandmothers"!

Clearly, Dr. Gosden's work is an attempt to recover some "good" (via the tissue transplantation to cure a health disorder) out of the "evil" (the abortion). But, this is deceptive thinking as no real good can come from the murder of unborn babies. Society and the Church must speak out against this technology. Some alternatives to this technology exist and further biomedical research must seek out other alternatives. Sadly, this technology will only further dehumanize the unborn and later confuse abortion recipients and adoptees conceived from fetal ova.

"The ovaries of aborted fetuses procured by the most rigorous medical, ethical, and legal standards are a . . . morally justifiable source of potential personhood."

Using Aborted Fetal Ovary Tissue Is Ethical

Jonathan M. Berkowitz

Jonathan M. Berkowitz is a pathologist at Mount Sinai Medical Center in New York City. In the following viewpoint, Berkowitz argues that fetal ovary transplantation—a proposed procedure in which ovarian tissue from aborted fetuses would be implanted into sterile women—is ethical. He maintains that many of the concerns about fetal ovary transplants are unwarranted. If rigorous standards are followed, Berkowitz maintains, using aborted fetal ovarian tissue to help infertile women become pregnant is morally justified.

As you read, consider the following questions:

1. In the author's opinion, why is the contention that fetal ovary transplants break a natural law of biology a weak argument?
2. What are the two conditions that must be met in order for a fetal egg child to accept the circumstances of its birth, according to Berkowitz?
3. What is behind the resistance to fetal ovary transplants, in the author's view?

Reprinted from Jonathan M. Berkowitz, "Mummy Was a Fetus: Motherhood and Fetal Ovarian Transplantation," *Journal of Medical Ethics* 21: 298-304 (October 1995). Reprinted by permission of the publisher, BMJ Publishing Group, London.

> Who ran to help me when I fell,
> And would some pretty story tell,
> Or kiss the place to make it well?
> My mother

Ann Taylor, 'My Mother'

For most of us the word 'mother' is special. She is the person who gave birth to you, raised you, fed you, loved you, fought with you, and in the final analysis, did her best to be a good mother. For millions of years children, regardless of who raised them, could be certain they had a mother who was once a living person. However, the concept of motherhood has been challenged by research from Edinburgh University aimed at transplanting the ovaries of an aborted fetus into an infertile woman. Fetal ovary transplantation (FOT) will produce for the first time, a child who will inherit the genes of a woman who herself never lived. For many these circumstances are most unsettling; a person whose genetic mother was never born contradicts the way people have been born for millions of years. . . .

There are concerns about how a child might react to the knowledge that his mother was an aborted fetus. To this objection it will be demonstrated that anxiety over potential emotional damage is unwarranted in light of the significant analogous history of children adopted in infancy and children produced via medically assisted conception (MAC). . . .

Continuing Our Evolutionary Heritage

Another argument advanced against FOT is that we are skipping a generation of evolution and thus 'breaking a natural law of biology', according to the Human Fertilisation and Embryology Authority (HFEA) in London. This is a weak argument as it fails to take into consideration the molecular basis of evolution. Evolution occurs when re-combined or mutated genetic material is passed from one generation to the next at conception. The genetic material in a fetal egg has already undergone re-combination and is arrested in an early stage of cell division till ovulation. At ovulation, which for some eggs may not occur for forty years, the ovum completes nuclear division and it is not till conception that a unique genome is created. It is important to remember that evolution can only occur if genetic material is passed on to progeny. If a fetus is aborted, it can never contribute to our evolutionary heritage as its unique genes are lost forever unless, of course, fetal ova are harvested and grafted into a live reproducing woman. Therefore, concerns about 'skipping a generation' are totally unfounded as abortion (ie, the death of the organism prior to procreation), represents an evolutionary dead end. . . .

[The HFEA and others] fear that increased demand for fetal tissue secondary to infertility treatment will 'encourage abortion'.

It is, however, questionable how many women would undergo this invasive and psychologically complicated procedure purely for the benefit of another woman. In fact, it has been argued that abortion for the purpose of harvesting fetal tissue is morally reprehensible as it shows a gross disregard for life. While there is extensive debate over whether or not a fetus represents 'human' life, there is little doubt a fetus represents a form of life which has the potential to become human. To prevent such abuse, legislation could be enacted prohibiting reimbursement for donated fetal tissue. There were approximately 1.59 million abortions performed in the United States during 1988. Millions of eggs could be obtained even if consent for fetal tissue donation were granted in only a small percentage of abortions.

Emotional Repercussions for Fetal Mothers

For most individuals, the woman who raised them is the same person who sweated in labour to give birth to them. That a child can be conceived from the egg of a female who never lived outside her own mother's womb is an idea so alien to ancient traditions that it demands scrutiny—an idea one Boston University ethicist claimed to be 'so grotesque as to be unbelievable'. While the moral outrage of some is expected, given the uniqueness of FOT, history offers ample precedent for similar genealogical circumstances.

Helping Infertile Couples

Dr. John Fletcher [an ethicist at the University of Virginia in Charlottesville] said most of the ethical qualms [concerning fetal ovary transplants] pale beside the good that can be done for infertile couples. For example, he said, even though a child might be troubled to learn that its genetic mother was an aborted fetus, the child would almost certainly rather have been born from a fetus's eggs than not to have been born at all.

"The idea that you would be filled with self-loathing if 50 percent of your genes are from the ovum of an abortus seems to me highly questionable," he said.

Gina Kolata, *New York Times*, January 6, 1994.

Children raised by adults other than their 'biological' parents have undoubtedly existed during most if not all of human history. Take, for instance, the familiar scenario of a child adopted in infancy who has no personal memory of her biological parents and, as has been standard practice in the past, will know little if anything about them. An objection raised against FOT is the potential reaction of progeny to the news that their genetic mother was an aborted fetus. This argument is flawed as it assumes children carry the cultural and intellectual baggage of adults. We are at intellectual and emotional ease with the ideas and technology to which we are born. Tension is created by the introduction of new ideas and technology which upset established norms. For example, that this paper was written on a laptop computer is mind-boggling to my mother while for my son who has been raised computer-savvy, this fact hardly deserves notice. Most will agree that children are not born with preconceived notions of morality; rather, a child's moral character results from interactions with significant others. Therefore, for the fetal egg child (FEC) to accept his special circumstances with minimal emotional trauma two conditions should be met. First, the FEC must be accepted by her family and significant others. Second, as K.D. Pruett recommends, the facts behind the child's non-traditional conceptual status should be disclosed in a 'well-timed and developmentally appropriate' manner. With these conditions met, the child's chances of accepting his special circumstances without significant difficulty are enhanced. This is not to imply there will be no negative reaction once a child learns of her special conceptual status. Certainly there may be many emotions associated with the knowledge of being conceived outside sexual intercourse. Studies of children produced through MAC have demonstrated both positive and negative associations. An Australian group reported no 'increase in psychosocial problems above that which might be expected in the population at large' in a series of IVF [in vitro fertilization] children between the ages of one and three. Another study concluded that 'the majority [of children produced via IVF] were performing above the norm for their chronological age' but were subject to 'a significantly higher incidence of . . . behavioral and emotional problems'. Compare this to the testimonial offered by Lillian Atallah, a 'test tube baby', when she said: 'Knowing about my AID (Artificial Insemination by Donor) origin did nothing to alter my feelings for my family. Instead, I felt grateful for the trouble they had taken to give me life'. . . .

Comparing Adopted and Fetal Egg Children

While adoption and MAC-created families may have an increased risk of dysfunction, their potential shortcomings certainly do not warrant avoiding the joy of parenthood. Fetal egg children will be similar in many ways to children who are adopted or created through MAC. While adoption and MAC are not without hazard, what seems clear is that these alternatives to family building are, in and of themselves, not detrimental to the child or the family. Rather, as Elinor Rosenberg argues, it is the family's 'ability to deal with the special challenges inherent in adoptive [or MAC] relationships' which ultimately determines outcome. Successful child development is dependent more upon the quality of parenting than the genealogical ties a child has with her parents. Given these considerations, concerns over the possible psychological ramifications of being a FEC are perhaps exaggerated.

Lastly, some have suggested that we can avoid all potential harm by keeping the child ignorant of its conceptual history. Though a discussion concerning 'right to know' theories is beyond the scope of this paper, given how bad human beings are at keeping secrets, honesty is indeed the best policy. Better this child know his special circumstances at an early age 'so the knowledge can be absorbed over a period of time as the child grows', as the New South Wales Infertility Social Workers' Group contends. 'Children and adults are less upset by what are presumed to be unpalatable facts than by the deception that is designed to protect them from the facts', maintains A. Clamar. . . .

Unwarranted Arguments

Our present knowledge of reproduction dispels much of the concern over introducing unforeseen chromosomal defects through FOT. There is no medical evidence which suggests that fetal ovaries or eggs are inferior to the eggs present in a healthy adult female. With the exception of heritable disease, it is irrelevant who the genetic or biological mother of a child is. In the case of adopted children, who are analogous to potential FEC, there is ample evidence in the literature that adoption in and of itself is not detrimental. Rather, the dysfunction observed in some families results from the dynamics of the family situation, not the adoption. Furthermore, given the success of adoption and the similarities of adopted children to FEC, one can reasonably conclude that concerns of psychological harm resulting from a child knowing his genetic mother was an aborted fetus are overestimated. Adopted children, like potential FEC, rarely know anything about their genetic parents and are raised by individuals who are genetically unrelated. While adoption may not be the ideal, . . . the persistence of this ancient practice illustrates its utility.

Much of the resistance to FOT stems from the procedure's novelty. Throughout the twentieth century many of our ideas as to what is possible and hence normal have been shattered. Think of the computer user, in 1980; his 64 KB monster sitting mightily on the desk, confronted by the 33 MHz, 200 MB laptop. Remember the uproar in 1978 with the birth of Louise Brown, the world's first 'test tube baby'. It is not hard to envision that once established, FOT and FEC will be one of many variations of MAC and will gain, according to A.J. Bonnickson, a well deserved 'measure of respectability'.

It is important to challenge the assumption of a right to procreate. We should be asking why, in a world which is increasingly populated, we continue to devise new means of introducing children. Should we use science to resolve all of nature's imperfections? Is infertility an 'imperfection' needing remedy? Is a fetus an ethically and legally legitimate source for eggs, ovaries, and other tissues? If we accept the premise that there exists a fundamental right to procreate, then the ovaries of aborted fetuses procured by the most rigorous medical, ethical, and legal standards are a viable and morally justifiable source of potential personhood.

Periodical Bibliography

The following articles have been selected to supplement the diverse views presented in this chapter. Addresses are provided for periodicals not indexed in the *Readers' Guide to Periodical Literature*, the *Alternative Press Index*, or the *Social Sciences Index*.

Marcia Barinaga — "Researchers Broaden the Attack on Parkinson's Disease," *Science*, January 27, 1995.

Stephen Chapman — "Tolerance of Abortion Leads to an Unsettling Future," *Conservative Chronicle*, January 26, 1994. Available from Box 29, Hampton, IA 50441.

Jon Cohen — "New Fight over Fetal Tissue Grafts," *Science*, February 4, 1994.

Sarah Glazer — "The Fight over Fetal Tissue," *Washington Post*, June 30, 1992. Available from Reprints, 1150 15th St. NW, Washington, DC 20071.

Jeff Goldberg — "Fetal Attraction," *Discover*, July 1995.

James J. Kilpatrick — "Fetal Research Receives Go-Ahead," *Conservative Chronicle*, April 29, 1992.

Gina Kolata — "New Evidence on Fetal Cells," *New York Times*, May 2, 1995.

Thomas H. Maugh II — "Pig Tissue May Aid Parkinson's Treatment," *Los Angeles Times*, November 1, 1995. Available from Reprints, Times Mirror Square, Los Angeles, CA 90053.

Robert M. Patrick and Eileen Rosen — "Creation 'for Research Only,'" *Human Life Review*, Winter 1995. Available from 150 E. 35th St., Rm. 840, New York, NY 10016.

Paul Ranalli — "Naturally Occurring Brain Chemicals Show Promise in Limiting Parkinson's Disease at Its Earliest Stages," *National Right to Life News*, February 22, 1995. Available from 419 Seventh St. NW, Suite 500, Washington, DC 20004.

Paul Ranalli — "No Breakthroughs Using Human Fetal Tissue to Cure Neurological Diseases," *National Right to Life News*, January 1995.

Janice G. Raymond — "Taking Issue with Fetal Tissue," *On the Issues*, Spring 1993. Available from PO Box 3000, Dept. OTI, Denville, NJ 07834.

D. Redman — "The Choices," *Mother Jones*, January/February 1994.

Cal Thomas — "Proposal Defines Down Humanity," *Conservative Chronicle*, October 12, 1994.

Traci Watson — "A Tissue of Promises," *U.S. News & World Report*, August 8, 1994.

For Further Discussion

Chapter 1

1. John Paul II maintains that because all life is sacred, abortion is always wrong, under any circumstances. Jerry Z. Muller argues that abortion can be a moral choice under some circumstances. Whose argument is stronger, and why? Does the fact that John Paul II is the head of the Catholic Church have any influence on your assessment of his argument? Explain your answer.

2. William Brennan contends that abortion is murder because it kills an unborn child. Don Sloan maintains that all killing is not murder and that calling abortion murder does not make it so. What reasoning do Brennan and Sloan use to support their arguments? In your opinion, which author presents the most compelling reasons? Explain.

Chapter 2

1. Ellen Goodman maintains that late-term abortion is an emergency procedure employed when a fetus is severely deformed or otherwise nonviable. Brenda Shafer contends that the late-term abortions she witnessed were tantamount to infanticide. Based on these viewpoints, would you support or oppose legislation that would ban late-term abortions? Why?

2. Sandra Day O'Connor, Anthony Kennedy, and David Souter argue that even though laws requiring a 24-hour waiting period for an abortion might result in a long delay for the woman, this delay is not an undue burden. John Paul Stevens contends that the 24-hour waiting period is an undue burden. All the authors base their arguments on differing interpretations of the Constitution. Which of the two viewpoints uses these interpretations more effectively? Explain your answer.

3. Adrienne T. Washington asserts that parents have the right to be informed of their teenage daughter's abortion. Jennifer Coburn maintains that most teenagers inform their parents of their pregnancy and seek their parents' counsel about their options. Those teens who do not inform their parents usually have a very good reason for not doing so, Coburn argues. Whose argument is more convincing? Why?

Chapter 3

1. Patricia Lunneborg gives examples of several women's experiences with abortion, while Faith Abbott compares the choices made by two women with similar backgrounds. How do the authors use these accounts to make their points? Which viewpoint does so more effectively? Explain your answer.

2. Kate Maloy and Maggie Jones Patterson tell the story of a couple who had decided not to abort their fetus if it was diagnosed with hydrocephalus but who did proceed with an abortion when they discovered their fetus had Down's syndrome. Do you agree with their decision? Why or why not? Support your answer with examples from the viewpoint.

Chapter 4

1. Lawrence Lader and Randall K. O'Bannon agree that RU 486 abortions require multiple trips to the doctor's office and can be very painful. Yet Lader maintains the drug is safe, while O'Bannon contends it is unsafe for women. Whose argument do you think is more convincing, and why? Support your answer with examples from the viewpoints.

2. Madelein Gray maintains that she suffered from post-abortion syndrome after aborting her fourth pregnancy. Nada L. Stotland is a doctor who contends that post-abortion stress is a myth made up by abortion opponents. Comparing the two viewpoints, do you accept Gray's contention that her feelings of depression and alienation were the result of her abortion? Why or why not?

Chapter 5

1. Carson Strong argues that using tissue from aborted fetuses for medical purposes is ethical because the benefits that can come from its use outweigh any unethical aspects of abortion. Mary DeTurris contends that trading the life of the fetus for another person's life does not justify using tissue from aborted fetuses. Whose argument is stronger? Support your answer.

2. Jonathan M. Berkowitz maintains that using ovarian tissue from aborted fetuses is ethical and that children born as a result of the transplantation would accept the facts of their birth. Lawrence F. Roberge foresees traumatic stress for the children born of fetal ovarian tissue transplantation when they learn of the circumstances surrounding their conception. With which author do you agree, and why?

Organizations to Contact

The editors have compiled the following list of organizations concerned with the issues debated in this book. The descriptions are derived from materials provided by the organizations. All have publications or information available for interested readers. The list was compiled on the date of publication of the present volume; names, addresses, phone numbers, and fax numbers may change. Be aware that many organizations take several weeks or longer to respond to inquiries, so allow as much time as possible.

ACLU Reproductive Freedom Project
132 W. 43rd St.
New York, NY 10036
(212) 944-9800
fax: (212) 869-4314

A branch of the American Civil Liberties Union, the project coordinates efforts in litigation, advocacy, and public education to guarantee the constitutional right to reproductive choice. Its mission is to ensure that reproductive decisions will be informed, meaningful, and without hindrance or coercion from the government. The project disseminates fact sheets, pamphlets, and editorial articles and publishes the quarterly newsletter *Reproductive Rights Update*.

Alan Guttmacher Institute
120 Wall St., 21st Fl.
New York, NY 10005
(212) 248-1111
fax: (212) 248-1951

The institute is a reproduction research group that advocates the right to safe and legal abortion. It provides extensive statistical information on abortion and voluntary population control. Publications include the bimonthly journal *Family Planning Perspectives*, which focuses on reproductive health issues; *Preventing Pregnancy, Protecting Health: A New Look at Birth Control in the U.S.*; and the book *Sex and America's Teenagers*.

American Life League (ALL)
PO Box 1350
Stafford, VA 22555
(540) 659-4171
fax: (540) 659-2586

ALL promotes family values and opposes abortion. The organization monitors congressional activities dealing with pro-life issues and provides information on the physical and psychological risks of abortion. It produces educational materials, books, flyers, and programs for pro-family organizations that oppose abortion. Publications include the biweekly newsletter *Communiqué*, the bimonthly magazine *Celebrate Life*, and the weekly newsletter *Lifefax*.

Americans United for Life (AUL)
343 S. Dearborn St., Suite 1804
Chicago, IL 60604-3816
(312) 786-9494

AUL promotes legislation to make abortion illegal. The organization operates a library and a legal-resource center. It publishes the quarterly newsletter *Lex Vitae*, the monthly newsletters *AUL Insights* and *AUL Forum*, and numerous booklets, including *The Beginning of Human Life* and *Fetal Pain and Abortion: The Medical Evidence.*

Catholics for a Free Choice (CFFC)
1436 U St. NW, Suite 301
Washington, DC 20009
(202) 986-6093
fax: (202) 332-7995

CFFC supports the right to legal abortion and promotes family planning to reduce the incidence of abortion and to increase women's choice in childbearing and child rearing. It publishes the bimonthly newsletter *Conscience*, the booklet *The History of Abortion in the Catholic Church*, and the quarterly *Conscience: A Newsjournal of Prochoice Catholic Opinion*, which serves as a forum for dialogue on ethical questions related to human reproduction.

Center for Bio-Ethical Reform (CBR)
PO Box 8056
Mission Hills, CA 91346
(818) 360-2477
fax: (818) 360-2477

CBR opposes legal abortion, focusing its arguments on abortion's moral aspects. Its members frequently address conservative and Christian groups throughout the United States. The center also offers training seminars on fundraising to pro-life volunteers. CBR publishes the monthly newsletter *In-Perspective* and a student training manual for setting up pro-life groups on campuses titled *How to Abortion-Proof Your Campus*. It also produces audiotapes, such as "Is the Bible Silent on Abortion?" and "No More Excuses."

Childbirth by Choice Trust
344 Bloor St. West, Suite 306
Toronto, ON M5S 3A7
CANADA
(416) 961-1507
fax: (416) 961-5771

Childbirth by Choice Trust's goal is to educate the public about abortion and reproductive choice. It produces educational materials that aim to provide factual, rational, and straightforward information about fertility control issues. The organization's publications include the booklet *Abortion in Law, History, and Religion* and the pamphlets *Unsure About Your Pregnancy? A Guide to Making the Right Decision* and *Information for Teens About Abortion*.

Human Life Foundation (HLF)
150 E. 35th St., Rm. 840
New York, NY 10016
(212) 685-5210
fax: (212) 725-9793

The foundation serves as a charitable and educational support group for individuals opposed to abortion, euthanasia, and infanticide. HLF offers financial support to organizations that provide women with alternatives to abortion. Its publications include the quarterly *Human Life Review* and books and pamphlets on abortion, bioethics, and family issues.

Human Life International (HLI)
7845 Airpark Rd., Suite E
Gaithersburg, MD 20879
(301) 670-7884
fax: (301) 869-7363

HLI is a pro-life family education and research organization that believes that the fetus is human from the moment of conception. It offers positive alternatives to what it calls the antilife/antifamily movement. The organization publishes *Confessions of a Prolife Missionary*, *Deceiving Birth Controllers*, and the monthly newsletters *HLI Reports* and *Special Reports*.

National Abortion and Reproductive Rights Action League (NARAL)
1156 15th St. NW, Suite 700
Washington, DC 20005
(202) 973-3000
fax: (202) 973-3096

NARAL works to develop and sustain a pro-choice political constituency in order to maintain the right of all women to legal abortion. The league briefs members of Congress and testifies at hearings on abortion and related issues. It publishes the quarterly *NARAL Newsletter*.

National Conference of Catholic Bishops (NCCB)
3211 Fourth St. NE
Washington, DC 20017-1194
(202) 541-3000
fax: (202) 541-3054

The NCCB, which adheres to the Vatican's opposition to abortion, is the American Roman Catholic bishops' organ for unified action. Through its committee on pro-life activities, it advocates a legislative ban on abortion and promotes state restrictions on abortion, such as parental consent/notification laws and strict licensing laws for abortion clinics. Its pro-life publications include the educational kit *Respect Life* and the monthly newsletter *Life Insight*.

National Right to Life Committee (NRLC)
419 Seventh St. NW, Suite 500
Washington, DC 20004
(202) 626-8800

NRLC is one of the largest organizations opposing abortion. The committee campaigns against legislation to legalize abortion. It encourages ratification of a constitutional amendment granting embryos and fetuses the same right to life as living persons, and it advocates alternatives to abortion, such as adoption. NRLC publishes the brochure *When Does Life Begin?* and the periodic tabloid *National Right to Life News*.

Operation Rescue National (ORN)
PO Box 740066
Dallas, TX 75374
(214) 348-8866
fax: (214) 907-0277

ORN conducts abortion clinic demonstrations in large cities across the country. It pickets abortion clinics, stages clinic blockades, and offers sidewalk counseling in the attempt to persuade women not to have abortions. ORN publishes the quarterly *Operation Rescue National Newsletter* and disseminates a variety of pro-life brochures, pamphlets, and other materials.

Planned Parenthood Federation of America (PPFA)
810 Seventh Ave.
New York, NY 10019
(212) 541-7800
fax: (212) 245-1845

PPFA is a national organization that supports people's right to make their own reproductive decisions without governmental interference. It provides contraception, abortion, and family planning services at clinics located throughout the United States. Among its extensive publications are the pamphlets *Abortions: Questions and Answers*, *Five Ways to Prevent Abortion*, and *Nine Reasons Why Abortions Are Legal.*

Post Abortion Ministries (PAM)
PO Box 281463
Memphis, TN 38168-1463
(901) 837-3343

PAM is a nondenominational Christian educational outreach program. The organization provides materials to train, educate, and motivate Christians to counsel individuals dealing with the aftermath of abortions. It publishes a variety of brochures, booklets, and other materials as well as the quarterly *Set Free . . .*, which focuses on issues related to post-abortion trauma.

Pro-Life Action League
6160 N. Cicero Ave., Suite 600
Chicago, IL 60646
(312) 777-2900
fax: (312) 777-3061

The league's purpose is to prevent abortions through legal, nonviolent means. It advocates the prohibition of abortion through a constitutional amendment. It conducts demonstrations against abortion clinics and other agencies involved with abortion. The league produces videotapes and publishes various brochures, the book *Closed: 99 Ways to Stop Abortion*, and the quarterly newsletter *Pro-Life Action News*.

Religious Coalition for Reproductive Choice (RCRC)
1025 Vermont Ave. NW, Suite 1130
Washington, DC 20005
(202) 628-7700
fax: (202) 628-7716

RCRC consists of more than thirty Christian, Jewish, and other religious groups committed to enabling individuals to make decisions concerning abortion in accordance with their conscience. The organization supports abortion rights, opposes antiabortion violence, and educates policy makers and the public about the diversity of religious perspectives on abortion. RCRC publishes booklets, an educational essay series, the pamphlets *Abortion and the Holocaust: Twisting the Language* and *Judaism and Abortion*, and the quarterly *Religious Coalition for Reproductive Choice Newsletter.*

Bibliography of Books

Randy Alcorn · *Pro Life Answers to Pro Choice Arguments.* Sisters, OR: Multnomah Books, 1992.

Robert M. Baird and Stuart E. Rosenbaum, eds. · *The Ethics of Abortion: Pro-Life vs. Pro-Choice.* Rev. ed. Buffalo: Prometheus Books, 1993.

Angela Bonavoglia, ed. · *The Choices We Made: Twenty-five Women and Men Speak Out About Abortion.* New York: Random House, 1991.

Miriam Claire · *The Abortion Dilemma: Personal Views on a Public Issue.* New York: Plenum Press, 1995.

Ruth Colker · *Abortion and Dialogue: Pro-Choice, Pro-Life, and American Law.* Bloomington: Indiana University Press, 1992.

Gary Crum and Thelma McCormack · *Abortion: Pro-Choice or Pro-Life?* Washington, DC: American University Press, 1992.

Mark Crutcher · *Lime 5: Exploited by Choice.* Denton, TX: Life Dynamics, 1996.

Barbara Duden · *Disembodying Women: Perspectives on Pregnancy and the Unborn.* Cambridge, MA: Harvard University Press, 1993.

Ronald M. Dworkin · *Life's Dominion: An Argument About Abortion, Euthanasia, and Individual Freedom.* New York: Knopf, 1993.

Anne Eggebroten, ed. · *Abortion—My Choice, God's Grace: Christian Women Tell Their Stories.* Pasadena, CA: New Paradigm Books, 1994.

Joseph Lapsley Foreman · *Shattering the Darkness: The Crisis of the Cross in the Church Today.* Montreat, NC: Cooling Spring Press, 1992.

David J. Garrow · *Liberty and Sexuality: The Right to Privacy and the Making of* Roe v. Wade. New York: Macmillan, 1994.

Sue Hertz · *Caught in the Crossfire: A Year on Abortion's Front Line.* Englewood Cliffs, NJ: Prentice Hall, 1991.

Sumi Hoshiko · *Our Choices: Women's Personal Decisions About Abortion.* Binghamton, NY: Harrington Park Press, 1993.

Carole Joffe · *Doctors of Conscience: The Struggle to Provide Abortion Before and After* Roe v. Wade. Boston: Beacon Press, 1995.

Donald P. Judges	*Hard Choices, Lost Voices: How the Abortion Conflict Has Divided America, Distorted Constitutional Rights, and Damaged the Courts.* Chicago: Ivan R. Dee, 1993.
Frances Myrna Kamm	*Creation and Abortion: A Study in Moral and Legal Philosophy.* New York: Oxford University Press, 1992.
Andrew Kimbrell	*The Human Body Shop: The Engineering and Marketing of Life.* San Francisco: Harper, 1993.
Pam Koerbel	*Abortion's Second Victim.* Rev. ed. Chattanooga, TN: AMG Publishers, 1991.
Lawrence Lader	*A Private Matter: RU 486 and the Abortion Crisis.* Amherst, NY: Prometheus Books, 1995.
Lawrence Lader	*RU 486: The Pill That Could End the Abortion Wars and Why American Women Don't Have It.* Reading, MA: Addison-Wesley, 1991.
J. William Langston and Jon Palfreman	*The Case of the Frozen Addicts.* New York: Pantheon Books, 1995.
Philip Lawler	*Operation Rescue: A Challenge to the Nation's Conscience.* Huntington, IN: Our Sunday Visitor Press, 1992.
Patricia W. Lunneborg	*Abortion: A Positive Decision.* New York: Bergin & Garvey, 1992.
David Mall, ed.	*When Life and Choice Collide: Essays on Rhetoric and Abortion.* Libertyville, IL: Kairos Books, 1994.
Kate Maloy and Maggie Jones Patterson	*Birth or Abortion? Private Struggles in a Political World.* New York: Plenum Press, 1992.
Michael T. Mannion, ed.	*Post-Abortion Aftermath.* Kansas City, MO: Sheed & Ward, 1994.
Steven Maynard-Moody	*The Dilemma of the Fetus: Fetal Research, Medical Progress, and Moral Politics.* New York: St. Martin's Press, 1995.
Norma McCorvey with Andy Meisler	*I Am Roe: My Life, Roe v. Wade, and Freedom of Choice.* New York: HarperCollins, 1994.
Michelle McKeegan	*Abortion Politics: Mutiny in the Ranks of the Right.* New York: Free Press, 1992.
Elizabeth Mensch and Alan Freeman	*The Politics of Virtue: Is Abortion Debatable?* Durham, NC: Duke University Press, 1993.
Ellen Messer and Kathryn E. May	*Back Rooms: Voices from the Illegal Abortion Era.* Buffalo: Prometheus Books, 1994.
Patricia G. Miller	*The Worst of Times.* New York: HarperCollins, 1993.

Harold J. Morowitz and James S. Trefil — *The Facts of Life: Science and the Abortion Controversy.* New York: Oxford University Press, 1992.

Marvin Olasky — *A Social History of Abortion in America.* Wheaton, IL: Crossway Books, 1993.

Eric Pastuszek — *Is the Fetus Human?* Rockford, IL: Tan Publishers, 1993.

Suzanne Rini — *Beyond Abortion: A Chronicle of Fetal Experimentation.* Rockford, IL: Tan Publishers, 1993.

Lawrence F. Roberge — *The Cost of Abortion: An Analysis of the Social, Economic, and Demographic Effects of Abortion in the United States.* LaGrange, GA: Four Winds Publications, 1995.

Roger Rosenblatt — *Life Itself: Abortion in the American Mind.* New York: Random House, 1992.

Eva R. Rubin, ed. — *The Abortion Controversy: A Documentary History.* Westport, CT: Greenwood Press, 1994.

Lewis M. Schwartz — *Arguing About Abortion.* Belmont, CA: Wadsworth, 1993.

Don Sloan with Paula Hartz — *Abortion: A Doctor's Perspective/A Woman's Dilemma.* New York: Donald I. Fine, 1992.

Rickie Solinger — *The Abortionist: A Woman Against the Law.* New York: Free Press, 1994.

Lloyd Steffan — *Life/Choice: The Theory of Just Abortion.* Cleveland: Pilgrim Press, 1994.

Bonnie Steinbock — *Life Before Birth: The Moral and Legal Status of Embryos and Fetuses.* New York: Oxford University Press, 1992.

Randall A. Terry — *Operation Rescue.* Springdale, PA: Whitaker House, 1988.

Randall A. Terry — *Why Does a Nice Guy Like Me Keep Getting Thrown in Jail?* Lafayette, LA: Huntington House, 1993.

Oliver Trager, ed. — *Abortion: Choice and Conflict.* New York: Facts On File, 1993.

Laurence H. Tribe — *Abortion: The Clash of Absolutes.* Rev. ed. New York: Norton, 1992.

U.S. Senate Committee on Labor and Human Resources — *Finding Medical Cures: The Promises of Fetal Tissue Transplantation Research.* Washington, DC: U.S. Government Printing Office, 1992.

Jeanette Vought   *Post-Abortion Trauma: Nine Steps to Recovery.*
                          Grand Rapids, MI: Zondervan, 1991.

Sara Ragle Weddington *A Question of Choice.* New York: Penguin, 1993.

Peter S. Wenz   *Abortion Rights as Religious Freedom.* Philadel-
                        phia: Temple University Press, 1992.

Kathleen Winkler   *When the Crying Stops: Abortion, the Pain and the
                        Healing.* Milwaukee: Northwestern Publishing
                        House, 1992.

Index